PRAISE FOR *A BOY, AN ORPHANGE, A CUBAN REFUGEE*

"Those of us who came of age in the turbulent times of the 1960s remember one of the most popular folk songs was "Guantanamera," written by the nineteenth-century Cuban freedom fighter José Martí. We sang, "Yo soy un hombre sincero de donde crece la palma." In this memoir of a nine-year-old "sincere boy from the land where palm trees grow," we are treated to the faith, hope, and love of every refugee, every migrant, on this troubled planet. We are reminded of our own immigrant backgrounds, our own ancestors, who endured the sadness and the fear—yes, the terror—of being suddenly uprooted from home and cast abroad to other shores, other tongues, other climates, other cultures. Another Cuban song, "Cuando Salí de Cuba," laments leaving one's heart and one's soul there. This lad, on the contrary, brought his heart and his soul with him and, like all immigrants, enriched our nation with his "joie de vivre," his humor, and his human spirit. Just like the fourteen-year-old boy who was my father, who arrived here from Sicily in 1904 after the death of his father.

"Tony Dora tells his own story of the first year of escape from Communist Cuba, but it echoes the story of millions of our race who have been caught in the endless migration of humans, animals, and plants that compose the story of life on earth. He speaks eloquently of the impermanence of the human condition, but his untold story is that of the permanence of the human spirit and of life itself, which paradoxically perdures to enrich all life on earth, despite the catastrophic change that continues throughout time."

—Sal Umana, Author of *The Twin Towers Trilogy* and
Entering Eternity with Ease
salumana.com

"It's not often that a memoir of someone you have never met invites you so quickly into their world and perspective. Both gripping and heartfelt, Mr. Dora's reflections on his Peter Pan childhood is a tale for the ages. Not only is it a window into his world, it also has a message for refugees (and the American Refugium) of today. While his story begins with heart wrenching circumstances, it ends (as few memoirs do) with such hope and brilliance and positivity. *A Boy, an Orphanage, a Cuban Refugee: The Road to Freedom* is both a history lesson and a love letter to life."

—Daniel Francis, Author of *Class Is (Always) In Session: Certain Thoughts During Uncertain Times*

"Of the 14,048 possible stories of the unaccompanied children of Operation Pedro Pan, Mr. Dora shares his heart-warming experiences assimilating from life in Cuba to an orphanage in Indiana in a charming manner through the innocent eyes of a 10-year-old."

—Yvonne M. Conde, Author of *Operation Pedro Pan-The Untold Exodus of 14,048 Cuban Children* and Editor of *La Sabiduría de los Nuestros*

"Tony Dora tells his story in the voice of a young innocent boy and his sister who, being sent from Cuba to America without their parents, ended up in an orphanage. The voice is so true we can feel his fears and triumphs as if we were there with him. This memoir is so well written, I couldn't put it down until I finished it."

—Florence Tannen, Author of *Momma's Black Refrigerator*

"Tony Dora's *A Boy, an Orphanage, a Cuban Refugee* is a warm and affectionate telling of his first months in a free country, the United States of America. Tony and his sister were among the Cuban children brought to the US in Operation Pedro Pan. While living in a Catholic-run orphanage in Vincennes, Indiana, Tony learned English, protected his sister, Norma, and himself from bullies, and kept in touch with his mother, who was still in Cuba. He also discovered he had little talent for an Indiana passion, basketball. While lonely and struggling to adjust to a different culture, this young boy remained cheerful and always grateful for being in a free country. Tony has an amazing ability to recall events that happened when he was two and three years old. As a transplanted Hoosier, I was pleased to read how welcoming and supportive the people of the Vincennes area were to the children in the orphanage."

—Larry McCoy, Author of *Everyone Needs an Editor (Some of Us More Than Others)* and Others

"'Nothing lasts forever,' Tony Dora writes toward the end of *A Boy, an Orphanage, a Cuban Refugee*. After twenty-three years, he had returned to the site of the Indiana orphanage where he spent twelve months as a young recipient of Operation Pedro Pan to find it gone. But decidedly not gone are his vivid memories of navigating a strange country and a new language very much on his own. This is a remarkable memoir of hope and resilience told with both a child's innocence and an adult's insight."

—Barbara Novack, Writer-in-Residence, Molloy University, Author of Pulitzer-Prize-Nominated Novel *J. W. Valentine* and Eight Books of Poetry

"I've been waiting to read this book since I first heard about the Pedro Pan children. Tony's story speaks to his resiliency and positive attitude; his faith and sense of humor are evident throughout the book. As a nine-year-old he was in a new country and ready for an adventure—requesting to go somewhere with snow. Enjoyable story that shows how parents, the US, and the Catholic church worked to save over 14,000 children."

—Jeanneen Bellows, Volunteer with Grow Up Great, Cub Scouts, and Boy Scouts

"In *A Boy, an Orphanage, a Cuban Refugee*, Tony Dora touchingly recounts his flight at the age of nine with his eight-year-old sister, sans parents, from a Communist police state to an unfamiliar foreign land, echoing the horrific plight of millions of refugees who, like him and his sister, found themselves entrapped in a tenuous exodus for survival. Dora speaks powerfully of the fragility of our worlds, the durability of the human spirit, and the sanctity of life itself. *A Boy* is a memoir that will inspire readers to recalibrate their values and revisit their gratitude for what they have."

—Michael J. Coffino, Award-Winning Author of *Truth Is in the House*.

"A wonderful book that chronicles the journey of a little boy to an unfamiliar world. The story will make you laugh and cry as you read about his encounters with a colorful array of characters who test his resilience and determination."

—Dr. Kenneth Lord, Lecturer in Computer Science, Queens College, CUNY, and Music Director of St. Andrew's Lutheran Church, West Hempstead, NY

"*A Boy, An Orphanage, A Cuban Refugee* places the reader squarely in the middle of a situation one may only have envisioned in the movies, or in the pages of history books. At only nine years old, in March of 1962, Tony sets off into the unknown with his eight-year-old sister, Norma. Possessing a keen mind, uncanny memory, a proud heritage, and the fierce love of a mother, Tony navigates them both through treacherous territory to America, away from the dark Communist regime of Fidel Castro. . . .

"Antonio and his sister represent those fortunate enough to receive positive treatment and education during their transition, as not all refugee children did. . . . Operation Pedro Pan would go down in history as an overall success for the futures of many Cuban refugee children. *A Boy, An Orphanage, A Cuban Refugee* is a descriptive and touching personal story of that success."

—Jan Moberg, Author of *Chaplain's Walk: Spiritual Side of Medicine*

"Where pure devastation and cultural burden was expected, Tony Dora befittingly shows how the innocence and sense of adventure of a young boy can create a heartwarming story."

—Julianne Haycox, Author of *Conversations with Grace*

"*A Boy, an Orphanage, a Cuban Refuge: The Road to Freedom* is a fascinating look at a part of history that many people might not be familiar with or [know] . . . existed. Tony Dora has expertly written about his and his sister's journey, fleeing Cuba and assimilating into life in the United States. This book is written with emotion and humility, and I think anyone with even a passing interest in Cuba and the plight of [those] thousands of children will find the book intriguing and enjoyable."

—John Reger, Author of *One with the Road*

"Tony's writing is inflected with a persistent buoyancy, notwithstanding the frightening depictions of life under Castro. The author fills detailed anecdotes of his year at the orphanage with reconstructed conversations that display humor and informatively illustrate the meticulous process of learning a new language and a new culture among the strangers who became his friends. There are poignant, teary moments of melancholy and reminiscences of the father he lost to leukemia when he was just four, but Tony focuses primarily on the comfort he found in the compassion of the nuns who taught and cared for the children. Despite a few too many basketball stories, this book delivers an enjoyable immigration story with a uniquely positive perspective. A tender, illuminating, upbeat valentine to the Operation Pedro Pan rescuers."

—*Kirkus Reviews*

A Boy, an Orphange, a Cuban Refugee: The Road to Freedom
by Tony Dora

© Copyright 2023 Tony Dora

ISBN 978-1-64663-879-6

All rights reserved. No part of this publication may be reproduced,
stored in a retrieval system, or transmitted in any form or by any means—
electronic, mechanical, photocopy, recording, or any other—
except for brief quotations in printed reviews,
without the prior written permission of the author.

Published by

3705 Shore Drive
Virginia Beach, VA 23455
800-435-4811

A BOY, AN ORPHANAGE, A CUBAN REFUGEE

The Road to Freedom

TONY DORA

VIRGINIA BEACH
CAPE CHARLES

"Operación Pedro Pan"—silkscreen by Tony Dora

*This work is dedicated to the parents
of all Pedro Pan children, especially to my mother,
whose selfless sacrifice made this exodus into safety
from Fidel Castro's repressive regime
and police state a reality.*

*And a special message to all Pedro Pan children
—yes, all 14,048 of us:
We will forever be brothers and sisters.*

TABLE OF CONTENTS

Part One: Leaving 1

Chapter I: Don't Disagree with Them 3
Chapter II: The Ides of March 15
Chapter III: Florida City 22
Chapter IV: Origins 36

Part Two: Journey into the Unknown 51

Chapter V: Saint Vincent's Orphanage 53
Chapter VI: May 70

Photos 83

Part Three: Cultivo una Rosa Blanca 91

Chapter VII: A Saber-Toothed Tiger Tooth! 110
Chapter VIII: Summer 119
Chapter IX: Autumn 143
Chapter X: Snow! 164
Chapter XI: Thanksgiving 172
Chapter XII: A New Year 181
Chapter XIII: Eleven 196

Part Four: Impermanence 205

Chapter XIV: Nothing Lasts Forever 207
Chapter XV: Reunion 216

Epilogue 222
Acknowledgments 225
Author Biography 226
Appendix 227

AUTHOR'S NOTE

People have often wondered how it was possible that Fidel Castro had no idea that so many unaccompanied refugee children were leaving Cuba. The truth is that he knew. He wanted to rid himself of what he termed the *bourgeoisie*—that is, the middle class; those who were, in his opinion, overly concerned with material possessions. Nothing pleased him more than to break up middle-class families and have those children separated from their loved ones.

As I look back on this period, I am astounded at the epic journey undertaken and what was accomplished by the work and sacrifice of so many selfless, dedicated people and organizations, such as Monsignor Bryan O. Walsh, director of Catholic Charities; the State Department of the United States of America; and myriad individuals who have remained nameless. I can honestly describe this epoch in my life as an adventure—a wonderful, miraculous adventure. I had the great fortune to be a Pedro Pan kid!

How can I ever offer my gratitude? Who can I thank?

If anything, this book is an effort to thank those individuals who helped me embark on this marvelous adventure.

April 29, 2022

Sixty-sixth anniversary of my father's death

DISCLAIMER

The dialogue has been reconstructed as best as I can remember. Some of the characters are a combination of the various persons I encountered in this journey, and the tone affirms my experience.

Although I have fictionalized some of the events, I have written them as my memory recalls them. Naturally, I have employed literary and artistic license. Furthermore, I have tried to intertwine dialogue and reflection. I believe that dialogue can be informative, compelling, and entertaining.

With the exception of historical figures and my family members (my parents, Tía Elvira, my sister, and me), the names have been changed.

PART ONE

Leaving

*Whoever survives a test,
whatever it may be,
must tell the story.
That is their duty.*

Elie Wiesel

CHAPTER 1

Don't Disagree with Them

I became a man when I was nine. My other option was death.

I didn't know it then, but the fact was that we had to leave Cuba.

"Now, remember what I told you. Don't disagree with them, and don't let them see you crying. Be polite. Say 'yes sir' or 'yes ma'am.' Don't make faces, and don't raise your eyes to the ceiling." My mom looked deeply into my eyes. "Do you understand, Juan Antonio?"

She never called me by my first and second names unless it was very important. Otherwise, I was just Tony. I nodded. She hugged me and added, "You have to be strong for Normita." She was referring to my little sister, Norma, using the diminutive, which means "little Norma."

And so began our journey to the United States—two little kids without their parents.

Our mother prepared us by telling us that we would be going on an "adventure"—that we would be meeting wonderful children like ourselves and making lots of new friends. We were going to a nice place, and *they* would take good care of us. We weren't sure who *they* were, but we were told that *they* were very nice people. My mother also assured us that we would all be reunited within a short time. It was just the three of us: Mom, Norma, and me. Our dad had passed away six years before, from leukemia.

"After all," she added, "this Communist regime cannot last much longer."

In reality, *they* turned out to be the State Department of the United States and the Catholic Welfare Bureau. The year was 1962. John Fitzgerald Kennedy was president, an avowed anti-Communist. And we were as well. Yes, we—two little kids, eight and nine years old—were avowed anti-Communists and political refugees.

We were just kids! How could we be political refugees?

⊙ ⊙ ⊙

A POLICE STATE

Why would parents send their children, unescorted, to a foreign country where a different language is spoken, with no guarantee that they would ever see each other again?

Our mom was about to explain why.

She searched in her purse and took out a newspaper article. "I got this from the underground."

"The underground?" I asked.

"You know, the people we know at church."

"Oh!" I still wasn't sure what the underground meant, but I sensed that this was very important.

"What I am about to read to you can get us into a lot of trouble if the wrong people were to hear us." She was whispering. "This is scary, Tony. It may frighten you, but you need to know what's going on."

She motioned to me to stand up. "Look at you! You will soon be ten years old, Tony! You're growing up, my child—and with that come responsibilities. You have to be a father to your little sister."

She asked me to sit, and she studied the newspaper article in her hand. "It says here, listen carefully, *Fidel Castro has turned the island nation of Cuba into a police state. There is no freedom. Everyone lives in fear.*" She paused and said, "Well, I think you know that. Don't you?"

"Yes," I said, scratching my head. "I think I do."

My memory took me to an evening—I must have been seven or eight years old—when two armed *milicianos* (the militia, Fidel's police force) rang my grandfather's doorbell. He and I were watching the news on television. Milicianos were asking around the neighborhood for donations to the revolution. When my grandfather said that he had no money, they forced their way into the house and followed him into his bedroom where he kept money in a chest drawer. They reached in and took all the cash he had there.

To add insult to injury, one of them brazenly counted the money, grinning to himself, as they exited the house. At least the other one had the decency to maintain an air of propriety—if he could really be given credit for that—by going about his business in a somber manner.

Soon after, the state confiscated my grandfather's business. My grandfather's firm was, as far as I could tell (my dad took me there once), a large carpenter's shop. His workers toiled making wooden crates called *huacales*. Mosaic tiles from Fábrica Mosaicos la Cubana—renowned for its mosaic tiles—would then be inserted into the huacales, which would, in turn, be driven to various construction sites in my grandfather's trucks. That's where my dad got his start—driving a truck for his own dad.

This was a business my grandfather had started from scratch when he was a young man. When they took it away, he was devastated. As if that were not enough, the state also confiscated the house.

And they froze his bank account.

◎ ◎ ◎

People who have never lived under a tyrannical ruler may find it difficult to understand that children are quite aware when the current political situation is ominous. I certainly was.

We children witnessed firsthand the tragedy our country was enduring. We observed it on the streets, in our schools, and on television. We saw people waiting for hours in line to buy food. Baldor, the private school that Norma and I attended, was taken over by the state, and Mr. Baldor himself had to flee the country.

The most dramatic of all was when Fidel's men held trials for Batista's soldiers and sympathizers. Fulgencio Batista was the dictator Fidel overthrew on January 1, 1959. The only proof of guilt needed was an accusatory finger pointed at a defendant. The sad truth is that all were deemed guilty, and all were executed immediately before a firing squad.

And all of this was broadcast on television.

So, yes, children were quite aware that these were perilous times indeed.

◉ ◉ ◉

My mom continued reading: "*In addition, food, clothing and medicine are rationed. People have to wait in long lines for hours to buy groceries, and they cannot buy any food they want. They can only get whatever is allotted to them or whatever is available. Sometimes the grocery store runs out of food.* You know that, too."

"Yes, I do, Mom. I have seen the long lines."

"*Speaking out against Fidel Castro's government is very dangerous—not only to yourself but to your family as well.*" She paused. "These are dangerous times, Tony. That is why the two of you . . . *we* have to evacuate this country! Do you understand?"

I looked at her in disbelief, stupefied.

"Let me continue." She looked at the article again. "*In order to curry favor with the authorities, some people spy on each other. No one can ever tell who is spying on them. No one can be trusted—not even one's own family.*"

She paused again and exhaled.

"That's the reason why we have to keep this a secret. We can't tell anybody that we are leaving." She resumed reading. "Now listen to this: *An atheist Communist indoctrination has swept throughout Cuba and is being taught in all schools. Children are brainwashed to spy on their own parents.*"

"Why is Fidel doing this?" I asked. "I don't understand."

My mother put the article down. "Neither do I," she admitted. "I don't know—because he's a Communist!"

"What else does it say there?" I pointed to the newspaper article.

"Yes, let me continue. *The most disconcerting and frightening of all is that Fidel Castro has announced that parents no longer have any say regarding the care of their offspring. Now every child in Cuba is the property—*"

"Property!" she exclaimed, interrupting herself. "As if you were cattle!"

She shook her head in disbelief. "*Now every child in Cuba is the property of the Communist state. From now on, the state will make all decisions concerning children and dictate whatever it wishes to do with them.*"

My mom looked at me. "Do you understand how serious this is?"

"I . . . I think I do."

"Does it scare you, my child?"

"Yes, Mom, it sure does!"

Her gaze was grave and serene at the same time. She held out her arms and embraced me.

◉ ◉ ◉

Generally, most parents will do whatever it takes to safeguard their children. No price is too steep. Thus, Cuban parents started secretly sending their offspring to the United States. My mom was one of them.

Parents deemed guilty of such a crime were imprisoned. Some were executed. She was willing to pay the price.

◉ ◉ ◉

"You're allowed to take a small bag." Later that day, Mom taught Norma and me how to pack our clothes. "A pair of pants and shirt, a nice dress for Normita, some socks and underwear, pajamas, slippers—"

"How about toothbrushes?" Norma inquired.

"*One* toothbrush," our mother intoned.

"Toothpaste and comb!" I quipped.

"Yes, of course. *One* of each."

"Can I keep my eyeglasses?" I was kidding. "You know I can't read without them."

"That's one thing about you that I'm going to miss, Tony." My mom gazed at me and smiled. "Your whacky humor."

"And toys!" I saved this one for last.

"No toys, Juan Antonio!" She used my first and second names again. *Oh boy, she must be really serious about not packing any toys!* I thought.

She went to gather up two small suitcases and placed them on the bed. "You need to learn how to pack your luggage. I'll teach you." She folded clothes as she spoke. "Remember the day we took you to get vaccinated?"

"Yes, of course."

"This is the reason why—so that you can go to the United States." She looked directly into our eyes. "You cannot tell anyone, not your friends and not our neighbors. Not your aunts and uncles! Not even Nana or Abuelo or your tía Elvira."

Nana was the name I used for my grandmother. *Abuelo* means "grandfather," and *tía* means "aunt." Tía Elvira was our grandparents' daughter.

The severity of the moment started to sink in. "When do we leave?" I asked

"Tomorrow morning. Early."

◉ ◉ ◉

From December 26, 1960 (the day after Christmas, during President Dwight Eisenhower's administration), to October 23, 1962 (during the Missile Crisis, while John F. Kennedy was president), 14,048 unescorted children left Cuba for the United States in what became known as Operation Pedro Pan. The US State Department was approached by Fr. Walsh and others to authorize visa waivers and funds. Fr. Bryan O. Walsh (a thirty-year-old Irish-born Catholic priest with a brogue who didn't speak a word of Spanish), was the director of the Catholic Welfare Bureau—later renamed Catholic Charities. And, on January 3, 1961, the Catholic Welfare Bureau was authorized by the State Department to waive visa requirements for the children.

The term *Peter Pan* was the creation of Gene Miller, a reporter with the Miami Herald. He was on a plane from Miami with five of the 50 refugees who went to Evansville, Indiana. He wrote, "*This is the underground railway in the sky—Operation Peter Pan.*" The term first appeared in his article of March 9, 1962, "Peter Pan Means Real Life to Some Kids."

◉ ◉ ◉

"Daddy went to Tampa six years ago," my mom continued, "before Fidel had risen to power, to scout the area so that we would move there. Do you remember?"

We nodded. How could we ever forget? Many years later, I found his American visa, dated on my fourth birthday.

"He stayed with Pablo and Gloria," my mom said, "but felt so sick that he returned within a few weeks. He looked so pale! We rushed him to the hospital. The doctors told us he had leukemia. He died *two weeks* after his return from Tampa and *two weeks* before his birthday. He would have been twenty-nine. Such a strong and healthy man. And he died! We buried him the next day." My mom shed a tear, and so did we.

It was customary in Cuba to bury your loved ones the day after their deaths.

"Your father was a very popular man. Everyone loved him. The whole family went to the funeral," my mother whispered. "The whole neighborhood went."

Except for Norma and me. We did not go to the funeral.

Instead, we were told that Daddy had gone back to Tampa and that we would soon meet up with him. Norma and I spent the day of the funeral with one of the neighbors. She gave us cake and ice cream and played games with us. In retrospect, I think that our mother's decision was a great one. We were too young to be subjected to the trauma of such a loss. I recall that whenever I saw airplanes flying above, I would exclaim, "¡Ahí viene Papi!" (There comes Daddy!) Two years after his death, our mom finally told us that he had passed away. By then we had become accustomed to his absence.

"This is how you fold your shirt and blouse." Our mom went back to teaching us how to pack our clothes. "Try it."

Our attempt at folding was a process of trial and error.

"And this is how you arrange them in your luggage."

We gamely tried that as well. She was so patient. I knew that she was trying to savor our company. For all she knew, for all *we* knew, we might never see each other again. This was the price of freedom. She was not alone. The parents of 14,048 children were making the same sacrifice.

Although I realized that this might be the last time we would ever see each other, deep down I did not believe it. I knew that, somehow, we would be together again. At least, I convinced myself that this would be so.

"Mami, the kids are going to the park, biking," I declared suddenly. Then I dared to ask, "May I go?" I didn't think she would say yes, but she did.

"Just don't tell any of them that you're leaving tomorrow," she said. "You simply don't know who's listening. For all you know, the *comité* could be watching."

The comité ("committee") was made up of people from the neighborhood. Its full name was the Committee for the Defense of the Revolution (El Comité para la Defensa de la Revolución). Every block had one. You could do nothing without their approval. If you wanted to visit your family in another town, you had to ask the committee for permission. If a friend or relative was going to visit you for a few days, you had to ask for permission. If you wanted to take up a particular career or apply for a job, you had to ask the committee for permission—

that is, provided that the government allowed you to pursue the career you desired. And then you had to be lucky enough to find a job in your chosen career, because such a job might not exist at all.

Frankly, the real purpose of the committee was for people to spy on each other. The Communist Party explained it as "a system of collective vigilance." Its members wanted to find out what every person on their block was doing and what relation each individual had with counterrevolutionaries.

As a result, no one could be trusted. Your own family could not be trusted. This could not be overemphasized. Furthermore, you could get into a lot of trouble just by expressing disagreement with the system.

I gained a lot of respect for my mother that day. She was willing to give up her time with us so that we could be with our friends. This was so common of Cuban parents during this historical period—the willingness to surrender their children for freedom, with no assurance that they would ever see them again. I felt torn and guilty for being so selfish. At the same time, I wanted to say goodbye to my buddies, without actually using the words. Being present to them was my farewell.

"It won't be long," I promised her, "just a couple of hours."

"That's okay," she replied, "and take Normita with you."

Biking in the park on our last day in Cuba was bittersweet. I had fun with my friends, but my thoughts were with my mom. My thoughts also reverted to Papi, our father. Our dad was a carpenter, plumber, mason, electrician. He built his brother's house in Guanabacoa, one of the suburbs of Havana. Papi's name was Félix Antonio, but everyone referred to him by his nickname, *Ñico*.

To pronounce the Spanish ñ, think of words like *niño, jalapeño, señor*. The Spanish letter ñ is pronounced in a similar way to the English words *tenure, aneurysm*, and *senior*—which is close to señor. Ñico is one of the nicknames for Antonio; there are several: Tonio and Tonino are popular—so is Tony, which is my nickname.

Our mom's name was Noadías, but everyone called her Nona.

People have often asked me about her unusual name. When she was born, her dad, who was a Seventh Day Adventist minister, gathered the congregation together in order to choose a name for his infant daughter. He opened a Bible at random and, while looking away, pointed to a spot on the page. When he looked down, he saw the name *Noadías*—Noadiah in English. The name appears in the sixth chapter of the Book of Nehemiah, verse fourteen. Nothing is known about Noadiah, except that she was a prophetess.

Later on, when she was a teenager, our mom converted to the Roman Catholic faith.

From the age of twelve, our dad worked for his father, driving a truck to countless construction locations. He may have been rather young to be driving a truck, but he looked quite grown-up, and nobody ever gave his age a second thought. At least, that's the story I've been told.

It was in his father's business that our dad learned to be a jack-of-all-trades. I would have learned so much from him. Today, sadly, I can barely hammer a nail. But even though I was only four years old when he died, I have lots of memories of my dad. Tía Elvira, my dad's sister, tells me that I have been blessed with a great memory. I remember once telling her about something that happened when I was a baby in the crib.

"There was a little yellow duck hanging above me. I would look at it, as I was lying on my back, and try to reach it."

"What? Impossible!"

"It's true, Tía. I would also raise my feet and try to touch my toes."

"Come on! You're putting me on!"

"Sometimes you would go to the crib, pick me up, and cuddle me."

"You remember that?" She looked at me incredulously. "How is that possible?"

"I don't know, Tía. It just is."

It's a funny kind of memory, though. I can recall events from my early childhood, but, as the saying goes, sometimes I'm hard pressed to tell you what I had for breakfast this morning.

My sister, Norma, has practically no memory of Cuba and recalls little of our first few months in the United States. Yet she tells me that she feels our dad's presence. She knows that he is there to protect her. How I wish I could feel his presence! But I don't. I guess I have to be content with my recollections.

As far as these recollections are concerned, some friends have told me that they find it difficult to believe that my memory goes back that far. But I've met other people who claim that they too remember events from when they were two and three years old. In fact, I went to college with a Pedro Pan girl who had been at both the Florida City camp and at Saint Vincent's Orphanage. Although our paths crossed twice in those days, I don't recall encountering her at either place. She was exiting the camp and the orphanage as Norma and I were entering them. However, she says that she met Norma. Norma, of course, can't make such an assertion. At any rate, this Pedro Pan girl and I had a conversation while walking on the college campus.

"You may not believe this," I said, "but my memory takes me back to when I was two years old."

"That's nothing," she said and made the following declaration: "My memory goes back even further than that."

"Really?" I was quite intrigued. "You mean that you remember things that happened when you were one year old?"

"Even further."

"Give me a break!" I found this a little hard to believe. "How far back?"

"To the time when I was in the womb."

"Yeah right!"

"I'm telling you, I recall being in the womb."

"Oh yeah? What was it like?"

"Quite comfortable. It's like I had my own little apartment in there."

"No way! I just can't believe that."

"It's true."

"Okay." I knew that she was kidding, but I had to think of a comeback question. "Well then, what did the interior of the womb look like?"

Her gaze pierced my eyes and, very nonchalantly, she responded,

"Pink."

So there you have it—memory is a funny thing. The Boogie Man story will corroborate that.

◉ ◉ ◉

THE BOOGIE MAN

I remember very vividly walking with my dad on the street one night. I was probably three years old. He picked me up and thrust me up on his shoulders. We were laughing and having a good time. Suddenly, I noticed a dark, electrical cylinder atop a telephone pole. I was terrified of these things and shrieked, "¡El coco!" Coco means coconut, but it is also a mythical creature that snatches and gobbles up disobedient children. El coco is pretty much akin to the Boogie Man.

My dad brought me down from his shoulders and cuddled me. He reassured me, "Don't worry, son, I'll protect you!" Then, holding me close to his heart and walking quickly, he whispered, "Patica, ¿paqué te quiero?" (Little leg, what do I want you for?) He's the only person I've ever heard use this expression.

Well, I wanted to use my legs to run away from danger!

Patica is the diminutive for *pata*—that is, "leg"—except that pata only applies to the legs of animals. It is used in a comical way when referring to a human leg. The correct word for a human leg is *pierna*.

CHAPTER II

The Ides of March

I woke up very early in the morning of March 15, 1962. I had barely slept that night, thinking about my upcoming adventure. I knew that winters were cold up north, but living in the tropics, I had no idea what that really meant. Snow was a magical element I had never experienced in Cuba. I relished the idea of living in a country where I could encounter it, envisioning it as a beautiful, white, fluffy cloud like the ones in the sky.

But I was still in Cuba. I opened the front door and peeked outside. I looked up and down the street, wanting to record this cherished location in my memory. *No snow here,* I thought.

Norma and I had lived, at different times, in three houses on this block. By that I mean three homes where we slept. We spent most of the time with our grandparents and their daughter, Elvira, in their house. In the morning, Norma and I went to school, and our mom went to work. After school, the bus dropped us off at our grandparents' house. When our mom returned from work, she would pick us up. The three of us would often have dinner with Nana, Abuelo, and Tía Elvira.

Another aunt and uncle, four cousins, and all of our friends also lived on this block.

To the left of our house was the pharmacy. Across the street was the rear of the medical center Quinta la Benéfica. To the right, also across the street, stood the little chapel where our mom used to take us to Mass on Sundays when we were little. When we were older, we went to the cathedral, where I was an altar boy.

I stepped outside and crossed over to the lamppost, placed my right hand on it, and bid it farewell. *I shall return,* I vowed. But I wasn't sure that I ever would.

Norma came up from behind and startled me. "Why are we leaving our country? Do you know?"

"Yes, I know why," I murmured, cautioning her, "We have to speak very quietly, Norma, in case the committee is listening. Fidel has transformed our island nation into a Communist dictatorship."

She looked at me quizzically. I tried to offer an easier explanation. "That means something really bad. But he's bound to be toppled any day now."

Well, that was the prevailing belief.

◉ ◉ ◉

"Fidel is a bad man, Tony," my mom had disclosed to me the previous year. I was shocked. The country had proclaimed Fidel and his revolutionaries as heroes. "What I am about to tell you has to be kept a secret." My mother was whispering so quietly that I had to draw close to hear. "Do you understand?"

"A secret?"

"Yes. Promise me that you won't discuss this with anybody—not even with the family, and certainly not with Normita. She's too young to understand."

"I promise," I responded. "But why keep it a secret?"

"We can't trust anyone! You never know who's in cahoots with the committee. We have to abandon the country, Tony. We're going up north."

"Up north?" That meant the United States.

"Yes, I'm making preparations right now."

◉ ◉ ◉

THE FISHBOWL

Our mom spoke softly. "Let's go, children. Our ride is here."

We left very early that morning of March 15, the Ides of March, at around four o'clock. A car was waiting outside. We dared not speak. The driver, a trusted colleague of our mom, took our suitcases and put them in the trunk. Norma, Mom, and I got inside. No other family members were present. My mom had kept our departure a secret until last night. But even those she told had no inkling we would be leaving this early in the morning.

As the car drove the route to the airport, I silently bid farewell to the buildings and houses we passed on the highway.

When we arrived at the airport, we were ushered into a waiting room—*la pecera*. The correct term for a waiting room is *salón de espera*, but Cubans like to give people and things nicknames. For example, Fidel was *el caballo*, "the horse." *Pecera* means "fishbowl" or "fish tank," a fitting nickname for the hot waiting room enclosed within three glass walls.

Passengers leaving for the United States were forced to wait eight or nine hours in that hot waiting room with no air-conditioning—a farewell present from the government for *los gusanos,* which means "worms." That's what Fidel called those who did not support his revolution. Thus, we were gusanos, and we used that term proudly.

Family members and friends would be outside la pecera, looking in, but we were not allowed to communicate with them; this could get us into big trouble. We were supposed to sit there and wait. All the while, the milicianos kept a close eye on us. It was eerie.

"I'm scared, Tony." Norma clutched my hand.

"Don't worry," I assured her. "It will soon be over."

Mom had made me promise to be strong for my little sister. So I used the same word with her that our mom had used: "It's an *adventure*, Norma! We're going to a very nice place, and *they* are going to take good care of us."

Within a short time, some friends and family showed up. They peered through the glass walls for a split second, for they knew that we could not make eye contact.

"The whole neighborhood is here!" Norma exclaimed.

"That's what it looks like," I replied, "but don't make eye contact."

Mom also peeked through the glass wall, put her index finger to her lips and lowered her eyes to remind us to keep quiet.

And just as quickly, she was gone.

◎ ◎ ◎

LUGGAGE INSPECTION

The *milicianos* started calling the passengers one at a time. Norma and I were separated for this exercise. When my turn came, I was ushered into an office. The man inside appeared enormous to a little kid like me.

"Put your suitcase on the table!" he demanded.

Our eyes met. He was the head of the committee on our block! We were both surprised to see each other.

"You? So, you're a traitor too, aren't you?" he sneered. "When you get to Yankeeland, tell them that Cuba is the greatest country on earth!"

"Remember what I told you." I heard my mother's voice in the back of my mind. *"Don't disagree with them. Be polite."*

"I said"—he repeated his words deliberately and irately—"tell them that Cuba is the greatest country . . . on earth!"

"Yes, sir." I nodded.

He observed me skeptically. "Open your suitcase!" he barked. "Let's see what you've got!"

As he went through my clothes, my Adam's apple bobbed. "You have two shirts!" he scowled. "You only need one!" He took my best shirt, a brand-new one I had not yet worn, and threw it into a bin.

He grinned condescendingly. "You just made a donation to our glorious revolution." His gaze was intimidating. "Do you have a problem with that?"

"No, sir," I responded.

Then it happened. He found my toy soldiers and jungle animals. They were about three inches tall, khaki green, and made of hard plastic.

These were not just any toy soldiers; they carried rifles and machine guns and bazookas. Some had bayonets and were poised in hand-to-hand combat. My jungle animals were leopards, panthers, gorillas, alligators, rhinos, and elephants. I also had, like the song from *The Wizard of Oz*, "lions and tigers and bears!"

Oh my! Well, it was my fault. Mom had warned us not to bring any toys, but the temptation was too strong.

"Toy . . . soldiers," he said in a calculatingly low tone, "and jungle animals! My sons will love these!"

My mother had prepared me for such a situation. Once again, I heard her voice in my mind. *"If they take anything away, let them have it. Don't ever complain! Always be polite! Do you hear me, Juan Antonio?"*

I gulped and looked intently at the monstrosity of a man in front of me.

"Well." I spoke slowly and as calmly as I was able to. "I hope that your sons will enjoy playing with my toys as much as I have."

He appeared stunned by my response. He tilted his head sideways and scrutinized me with curiosity, as if thinking, *This kid's out of his mind!* Then he laughed loudly.

◉ ◉ ◉

PAN AM

After being detained for several hours, we were escorted outdoors to the airplane, a Pan American World Airways aircraft. Airport employees were busy loading luggage.

The path to the vessel was lined by milicianos equipped with rifles and machine guns. I had become accustomed to their ubiquitous presence. They were everywhere and were always heavily armed, no doubt as an attempt at intimidation. Nonetheless, these milicianos could not put a damper on my feeling of exhilaration. I had never flown in an airplane, and by gosh, this was going to be an adventure!

We had to climb a long ladder to board the plane. Once inside, a stewardess led us to our seats. From the window we saw our relatives on the roof of the departing flights building, waving at us. Norma started to cry. I tried to be strong for her, but I couldn't help it. I cried too.

The teary-eyed stewardess motioned us to take our seats. She wiped her eyes with a hanky and handed us some Kleenex tissues. We nodded in gratitude through our tears.

"Let me help you with those," she said as she fastened our seat belts.

The other passengers, children and adults, spotted their loved ones waving goodbye from the same building and started to cry as well. Then the other stewardesses joined us. Everyone was sobbing and weeping.

The pilot's voice through the intercom system interrupted the somber mood. "Welcome aboard Pan American Airlines. This will be a short flight—forty-five minutes, give or take a few. It's a beautiful, sunny day in Miami."

The stewardess handed Norma and me brown paper bags, saying, "Just in case you need them," and walked away.

Norma looked at me quizzically, "Why would we need these?"

I shrugged. "I guess we'll find out soon enough."

We sure did, the instant the plane took off!

Within fifteen or twenty minutes, we heard the pilot's voice again. "We're flying over United States of America international territory. You are free!"

Everyone howled with joy. People started clapping and hugging and kissing each other. Someone shouted, "¡Viva Cuba libre!" (Long live free Cuba!) and all responded, "¡Viva!" Someone else started singing "Guantanamera," and everyone sang along.

Guantanamera means "the lady from Guantánamo." It's a famous Cuban song made popular in the United States by Pete Seeger, Joan Báez, the Sandpipers, and others. After that, we broke into the Cuban national anthem and other patriotic songs.

An interesting historical annotation is that the United States has maintained a military base in Guantánamo Bay since the Marines took control of it in 1898, following the end of Cuba's War of Independence against Spain—which in turn followed the end of the Spanish-American War. On February 23, 1903, the United States Navy signed a perpetual lease agreement with the newly independent government of Cuba for an annual fee of $2,000 in gold.

CHAPTER III

Florida City

When the plane landed, I looked through our window and saw busy airport employees loading and unloading luggage from and into different airplanes. *Gee, the United States looks just like Cuba!*

We were led to a bus, and several children got on it along with Norma and me. "Where did all these kids come from?" Norma wondered.

I shook my head. "They must have been on the plane with us. We just never noticed them."

The bus ride was uneventful—that is, I don't remember any of it. After about an hour or so, we approached a little town with a small fence. A uniformed man opened the fence, and the bus went through, then parked beside a building. Rows and rows of houses lined both sides of the street. Two nuns and a few laypeople awaited us. The nuns wore long black habits and large white veils.

One of the nuns greeted us with a smile. "Welcome to Florida City!"

"Your new home," the other one announced.

Because there were so many children, we were taken into different rooms. Norma and I entered a small office and were instructed to sit in front of a desk. There sat a woman with large eyeglasses. She glanced at us past some papers she held in her hand and said in Spanish, "You are Juan Antonio and Norma Eulalia. Am I correct?"

"Yes, ma'am," I intoned.

"Your last names are Dora Travieso. Right?"

"Correct again, ma'am."

She addressed Norma. "Young lady, you are eight years old. Is that right?"

"Yes, ma'am." Norma nodded.

She then addressed me. "Young man, you are nine years old. Am I right?"

"Ten years old," I corrected her.

"Ten years old? Really?" She peered at the papers. "According to my records here, you are nine years old."

"Well, sort of," I replied, "but I'm almost ten years of age."

"But you have not had your tenth birthday yet. Am I correct?"

"No. Not yet."

"Okay then, you are nine years old."

"Technically, I guess."

"Listen, I understand that you are in a hurry to grow up, but let me tell you," she said, smiling, "there'll come a day when you are going to wish that you were younger, at which point you will be subtracting years from your age, not adding to them."

"Old people say that all the time."

She chuckled. Then she took off her glasses and resumed in a serious tone. "Let's continue, shall we?" She put her glasses back and stated in a perfunctory way, "Your stay here will be temporary, until we are able to locate a more permanent accommodation for you. Do you understand?"

"Yes, ma'am," Norma and I replied in unison.

She fidgeted with her glasses. "You will soon meet your foster parents." She looked at each of us. "Boys and girls are separated, of course, but the two of you will be able to see each other every day. First, however, we have some business to attend to."

She extended a long sheet of paper to us. "We would like you to fill out this form. It will help us find a suitable and permanent place for you."

I don't remember the questions that were asked, except for one—the one that inquired what kind of climate we preferred. I turned to my sister and whispered, "Norma, put a check mark next to the one that says that we want to go to a place where it snows all the time."

I had no idea what I was getting us into!

When we were finished, we handed in the form. The lady with the large glasses demonstrated her kindheartedness and compassion. "I know that you're going through a difficult time. Leaving your parents and your country is a traumatic experience."

Norma wiped a tear with her hanky.

"Dramatic?" I inquired.

"Traumatic. Meaning, uh, difficult, painful. Yes, the word *dramatic* also works." She adjusted her glasses. "What I want to say is that we are here for you." She looked at Norma. "*I* am here for you. Anytime. Just come here looking for me or tell your foster parents that you want to see me."

Norma's tears flowed freely. The lady stood and held Norma affectionately by the shoulders. "Come, let's meet your foster parents. They'll take you to your new home and introduce you to the children with whom you will be living." She ushered us towards the door.

Norma moved to hug her, but she was too small to reach the lady's shoulders, so she put her arms around the lady's waist.

"Oh," whispered the lady, cuddling Norma warmly, "that's so sweet."

◉ ◉ ◉

Our foster parents were waiting for us in an adjacent room. The lady with the large glasses turned to Norma. "Remember what I told you." Then she turned to me. "I'm here for you."

She made the introductions. "Norma, these are your new foster parents, Mr. and Mrs. Flores, and, Tony, these are Mr. and Mrs. Blanco."

Our new foster parents hugged us warmly, and the ladies kissed us on the cheeks. Norma's foster mother said, "Call me Caridad." *Caridad* means "charity," in honor of Our Lady of Charity (Nuestra Señora de la Caridad del Cobre), the patroness of Cuba. Caridad is a very common name for Cuban girls.

My foster mother said, "You can call me Natalia."

Our foster fathers did not reveal their first names.

Caridad informed us, "Your new homes are just a short walk away. Let's get something to eat. You're probably hungry."

We weren't. We had lost our appetites during the flight, but politely, we went along. They took us to a building, beyond which was a tent. It was humongous! From a distance, it could be mistaken for a circus tent. I asked, "What's the tent for?"

Mr. Blanco said, "That's the chapel. A priest says Mass there every morning and, of course, on Sundays."

"We also hold meetings in that tent," offered Mr. Flores.

Inside the building was a large dining hall. Our foster parents directed us to a table, and we sat down. I can't remember whether we were served or whether it was buffet style. Nevertheless, soon we were eating. Well, our foster parents were eating. Norma and I hardly touched our food.

During the meal, Mr. Blanco, my foster father, informed us, "Each house in the camp is home to ten children your age. Well, that is the ideal. In reality, sometimes as many as sixteen or more children are housed in a home. They are all run by people like us, retired Cuban couples."

"The children, that's you," interjected Natalia, my foster mother, "will sleep in bunk beds."

"And you'll take turns doing chores," said Mr. Flores, Norma's foster father, "such as taking out the trash, washing dishes—"

"Menial housework," Natalia added. "You know, light dusting and sweeping."

"And you will write letters home," added Mr. Flores. "But you have to be very discreet. The Communists read every letter. Be very careful not to say anything that will compromise your families."

"As good Catholic children, you go to Mass every Sunday, right?" Mr. Blanco asked. We nodded.

"I was an altar boy in Cuba," I said.

"Good." Mr. Blanco smiled. "You can be one here, too. We need altar boys."

After the meal, our foster parents took Norma and me to our respective houses. Mr. Blanco introduced me to the other boys. "This is Tony, your new brother. Boys, go ahead and get acquainted, and when you're done introducing yourselves, show Tony our sleeping quarters." He motioned to one of the boys. "Alex, will you be so kind?"

I liked Alex immediately, maybe because Alex was also the name of my best friend in Cuba, who had left the island with his two brothers and parents a few months before our own departure. As with all of the children who left Cuba in those days, we only found out about their departure by virtue of their absence.

After chatting for a while with my house "brothers," the new Alex took me to a large bedroom filled with bunk beds. He put his hand on a top bunk. "This is your bed."

A top bunk! How lucky could I get? That was exactly what I wanted.

I hesitated for a moment. "Alex, what I really need right now is water." I pointed to my throat. "It feels dry as a bone."

Alex took me to the kitchen and pointed to the faucet. "We drink tap water."

I drank three tall glasses; I was really thirsty.

Sleep did not come easily that first night. I kept thinking of the events that had led us to this point, and I wept silently for fear of waking the others.

A memory of my mom came to me.

❂ ❂ ❂

WATER!

My mother and I were in our second-floor unit in a two-story complex of several attached apartments in the round, with a spiral staircase leading up from the first floor to the second floor. She was busy doing housework, and I was sitting on a little chair on the balcony overlooking the rotunda below. I must have been about three.

All of a sudden—and for no reason at all, since I wasn't thirsty—I started crying out for water. "¡Agua! ¡Agua! ¡Agua!"

My mother brought me a small glass of water, but I refused it. She looked at me quizzically and asked, "Well, do you want to take a drink or not?"

I did not answer. I just shrugged, so she took the glass of water back to the kitchen and resumed her housework.

I cried out for water again. "¡Agua! ¡Agua! ¡Agua!"

My mother returned to me with the small glass of water. Once again, I refused it. She said in a testy voice, "I'm leaving the glass of water on this little table next to you. When you decide to drink some, just take it." And she went back to her housework.

I realized that this could be fun! I thought, *Let me drive Mom crazy.* So I cried out for water again, with a little more drama this time.

My mother rushed over to me and handed me the glass of water, but I wouldn't take it. She brought the glass to my lips, but I just shook my head left and right, crying out, "¡Agua! ¡Agua! ¡Agua!"

She tried to pry my lips open, but I kept them tightly shut. The instant she removed the glass from my mouth, I went back to screaming for more. She exclaimed loudly, "What's the matter with you?" Boy, she looked riled up. "I'm giving you water! Drink it!"

But I just shook my head and said, "Nope."

She set the glass forcefully on the little table. "Here's the glass of water." She was livid. "Take it when you decide to have a drink." She crossed her arms and gazed at me. "All right, Juan Antonio?"

I shook my head and also crossed my arms. That got her even more riled up. She stared at me angrily for an instant. Then she shook her head, composed herself, and went back to her chores.

The little devil in me tempted me to repeat my little ploy. I knew that it was wrong, but, I am sorry to admit, I wanted to drive her nuts. So, I returned to my howling. This time I made it sound like I was desperate for water.

"For crying out loud!" one of the neighbors downstairs hollered. "Will you please give that kid some water?"

"Hey, you, upstairs!" another one bellowed. "That little brat of yours is driving us out of our minds!"

A concerned woman offered her services. "Nona, are you having a hard time, honey? Do you want me to give you some tips on how to care for a little one?"

Oh boy! This is fun!

My mother was beside herself. The poor woman didn't know what to do, and this episode was bringing her close to tears.

Suddenly, Diego, our good friend and neighbor and a very large man, appeared at the doorway. He pointed an angry finger at me and roared, "Stop it, Tony! Shut your mouth!"

I had never seen him so infuriated. He was scary! I stopped crying out for water immediately.

Diego suddenly looked awkward as he realized he was interfering in a domestic squabble. He looked at my mom apologetically. "I'm so sorry for intruding, Nona."

My mom looked at him and mouthed a grateful *Thank you, Diego.*

That evening, when my dad came home from work, he asked my mom, "What happened today, Nona? The neighbors were all in an uproar. They were complaining to me that Tony was driving them up the wall. He kept crying for water and you wouldn't give him any!"

My mom told him what had happened, and he chuckled. She placed her hands on her hips and glared at him, unamused. "It was not funny, Ñico!"

"Well," he replied, "maybe not at the time, but it sure sounds funny now!" He started laughing again.

She shook her head, but after mulling it over for a few seconds, she nodded and said, "Yeah, I guess you're right." And they both started laughing.

☉ ☉ ☉

That memory helped me fall asleep that first night in Florida City. But before I did, I remember hearing a lone train whistle in the distance.

When I woke up, I felt ill at ease. I wasn't ready for my new and unfamiliar surroundings.

Several camps in Florida accommodated the Pedro Pan children. The one in Florida City was no different from the others, in the sense that it appeared to have been thrown together quickly, in a makeshift fashion.

Florida was ill equipped for the Cuban children inundating the Miami area in wave after wave. It's understandable. By some estimations, only 200 children were expected, and in a little under two years, more than 14,000 arrived in Miami. The majority, 93 percent, were Roman Catholic. Between 500 and 700 were Protestant, while 396 were Jewish.

Protestant children were placed in Protestant institutions and foster homes. The Jewish children were placed in Jewish foster homes and orphanages under the direction of HIAS (the Hebrew Immigrant Aid Society) and the Cuban Hebrew Congregation of Miami, known as the Circle.

As the lady with the large glasses had informed us, the camp was supposed to be a temporary shelter until a permanent site was procured—one where we would go to school, learn English, and be Americanized.

◉ ◉ ◉

THE FIRST LETTER

My initial attempt at a handwritten letter was an immense effort, but I got the hang of it.

> *Dear Mom,*
> *How are you? We are fine.*
>
> *Me and Norma are doing real good in the camp. Everyone here is real nice, and everyone is treating us real good. Our foster parents are real nice, and the kids are real nice too. Tell us how you are doing. We miss you and pray that we are together again soon.*

Your son, Tony, and your daughter, Norma, too.
PS: We remembered to write RASA on the back of the envelope.

Mom had told us to add *RASA* to every letter, which stood for *Recomendado a* San Antonio (Recommended to Saint Anthony); that way, the letter would always be delivered without delay or negative incidents. We really didn't believe in this superstition, but we figured, *What the heck; it doesn't hurt.*

Mom wrote us back:

Dear Tony and Normita:
I've been writing this letter since you left but couldn't mail it because I didn't know your address. I miss you both very much, with all my heart, and pray that we can soon be together again as a family. Tony, your tenth birthday is coming up in just a few short days. You are growing up! This ordeal has thrust you into adulthood at a premature age. Be strong for your little sister. Ask your Guardian Angel to come to your assistance and guide you. Norma, listen to your brother as if he were your father.

Love and kisses,
Mom

◉ ◉ ◉

Norma and I did have the opportunity to meet on a daily basis. In the beginning, I served as her comforter. One day, when she was brokenhearted with grief, I said to her, "Norma, do you remember what Mom said in her letter? She said to ask our guardian angel to come to our aid and guide us."

Norma grew quiet and smiled faintly. However, such acceptance was temporary. She was still struggling with her pain.

In the early days, she was at times inconsolable. It seemed that I was failing in my attempts to relieve her anguish. At some point I gazed into her eyes and vowed, "I promise you, Norma, no matter what, I will always protect you." That seemed to assuage her somewhat.

She gradually adapted to our new circumstance, though it was a painful process. But who was going to comfort me?

◉ ◉ ◉

THIS CAN'T BE REAL

One day, I wandered off to be alone. I sat on a dead branch under a tree in an abandoned storage area where they kept rusted old trucks. There I felt safe enough to let my tears loose and cry my heart out. I searched in my pocket for a prayer card that I had found in the chapel and took it out. It was the eighteenth Psalm. I read the third verse over and over again: *God, You are my rock, my fortress, my deliverer.*

It was cathartic. I soon discovered that my tears had dried out. Well, somewhat. Still, I continued to frequent that spot. It was quiet and peaceful. One day, Alex was wandering in the same area. I tried to act naturally.

"Don't be ashamed, Tony. I come here, too. It helps me think. It's a great place to cry."

"I don't come here for that reason, Alex—not anymore, anyway. Frankly, I'm no longer able to cry. I just have this gut feeling that this isn't real. You know?"

As soon as the words left my lips, my eyes got misty, and a tear trickled down my face.

Alex acted as if he hadn't noticed my tear and damp eyes. "Yes, I feel the same way, but it still hurts."

"Of course it does!"

"You know, Tony, I can't cry anymore either. It's like I've cried myself out. Sleep is something else I can't do anymore."

"Thank God I have no problem sleeping. The thing is, when I think of my mom and my family, I get this feeling in my throat." I sighed.

"It's like a tightness, isn't it?"

"Yes! And my chest feels . . ." I tried to come up with a word.

"Heavy?"

"Why, yes!"

"Looks like we're feeling the same kinds of things."

"I knew there was a reason why we have become such good friends."

"Brothers. That's what we are."

I stood to face him, and we shook hands. "Brothers," I confirmed the sentiment, and we hugged each other. We continued to meet there. It was a great place to talk and share our feelings—a place to comfort and support each other.

◉ ◉ ◉

FIELD TRIP

"We are taking you on a field trip," Mr. Blanco proclaimed. "We're going to explore the town!"

The announcement was met with shouts of joy. Our foster mother proceeded to hand each of us a sparkling, silver, half-dollar coin! We were ecstatic.

If I was going to treat myself, I could think of nothing better than chewing gum. Under the Communist regime, gum was essentially nonexistent, and fifty cents was newfound wealth. A kid could do a lot of shopping with that kind of money in 1962! We invaded a candy store. There it was: chewing gum of all types and shapes—Chiclets, Juicy Fruit, spearmint, and bubble gum. And a new type we had never seen before fashioned in colorful strips.

"Look at those beautiful colors," I exclaimed.

"I gotta get me some of those!" roared one of the boys.

"Me too!" Alex yelled.

I bought a whole bunch. So did the other boys. The storekeeper was grinning from ear to ear, so happy to have so many customers that he offered us some free candy. We went back to the camp in a very happy mood.

"Is this a great country or what!" shouted one of the boys enthusiastically.

"Hooray for capitalism!" hollered another.

◉ ◉ ◉

BROWN SUGAR

In Cuba, it was not customary to have pepper on dinner tables. Every table had salt but not black pepper. At least, my family did not have it; neither did my friends and other people I knew. In Florida City, however, every table was set with salt and black pepper in transparent glass shakers.

One particular meal comes to mind—not so much for what we ate but for what transpired. The incident taught me not to mess with kids who were bigger than me.

A new big kid was assigned to our table. On his first day there, he noticed the presence of the black pepper. He asked, "What is that?"

The little devil in me made me say, "Brown sugar. Try some."

He looked at it suspiciously. "Brown sugar? But it's black."

"Oh, that's because in the United States, brown sugar is actually black." I glanced at the kids at my table and egged them on. "Isn't that so?"

They all agreed and nodded. "Oh, yeah!"

The new big kid was so intrigued by the brown sugar that he did not notice the wily grins. He placed a slice of white bread on the palm of his hand and said, "Here, sprinkle some of that on this."

As I was showering his bread with pepper, one of the kids said, "Mmm. It's yummy!"

Then Alex chimed in. "To die for!"

"Come on! Pour on some more!" The big kid spoke so loudly that the children sitting at nearby tables became aware of what was going on.

Another kid at my table declared, "It's delicious!" The others covered their faces to hide their sly smiles.

I shook more black pepper on his bread, but the new big kid wanted much more. He shouted excitedly, "¡Échale! ¡Échale más!" which means "throw"—or "slap"—more on.

So I unscrewed the cap off the pepper shaker, spread its contents on his bread, and urged him to take a bite. "Go ahead. Try it!"

The kids at my table were beside themselves, trying to keep from laughing.

The new big kid ogled his slice of bread, folded it in two, and stuffed the whole chunk in his mouth with relish. He munched on it for a few seconds. Then his eyes opened so wide they looked like they would pop out of their sockets. His face turned red, and he spit the entire thing out. It was disgusting! He started coughing and hacking, black pepper grains practically spewing out of his nostrils.

He grabbed a napkin and scrubbed his tongue with it. He shook his head to remove any bits of pepper grains on it, then snatched another napkin, dunked it in his water glass, and wiped the wet napkin on his tongue. Then, with another napkin, he blew his nose so raucously that it sounded like a foghorn.

The kids at my table and I could no longer control ourselves, and we broke out in laughter. The kids at the nearby tables were rolling on the floor. He was the laughingstock of the whole place!

The new big kid looked at me angrily and hollered, "I'll get you"—cough, cough—"for this"—hack, hack.

He grabbed the wet napkin he was holding, covered his nose with it, and finally sneezed. Without going into detail, let's just say that his face was a wet mess—and not just with water.

His blood-red eyes were menacing as he cursed me out. "You . . . you . . . you [so-and-so]!"

Except the words he used were much more colorful.

◉ ◉ ◉

A few days later, as I was walking down the street, I became aware that someone was running towards me from behind. It was the new big kid! Before I could turn around, his arm hooked around my neck and held me so hard that I was incapacitated. With his other hand, he smothered my face with a slice of white bread smeared with black pepper. He pushed me down on the ground, forced my mouth open, and stuffed the whole thing in it.

Now it was my turn to hack and cough and sneeze.

"Ha ha ha!" he mocked me. "I got even with you! You . . . you . . . you [so-and-so]!"

This time his choice of words was even more creative and colorful.

And that's how I learned never to mess with a kid who was bigger than me.

CHAPTER IV

Origins

One day, Mr. and Mrs. Blanco called a meeting. They sat on two chairs, facing us as we sat on three sets of couches in the living room.

Mr. Blanco opened the proceedings. "We have called you together to offer some information about what's going on in Cuba and why you are here."

Natalia added, "Some of you boys have approached us about this issue, simply because you don't quite comprehend what's going on."

"It's important that you understand the . . . how should I put it?" Mr. Blanco was searching for a word. "Well, the origins—yes, that's a good word—the origins of the situation. As you know," he went on, "Fidel Castro, along with three others—his brother Raúl, Ernesto Guevara, whom we call Che, and Camilo Cienfuegos—took over Cuba on the first of January, New Year's Day, 1959."

We nodded in agreement.

"This was a coup d'état against the government of Fulgencio Batista. I'm sure you know that, right?" Natalia said. We nodded again; every Cuban knew that! "What you may not know," Natalia continued, "is that Batista took control of Cuba—in an almost bloodless coup, mind you—on March 10, 1952, three months prior to the general elections."

Mr. Blanco interjected, "And that really pissed Fidel off, because he was running for Congress!"

"Lorenzo!" Natalia whispered, keeping her eyes on the floor. "Your language, please!"

Ah, so Lorenzo is his name! He had never divulged his first name to us. We would always refer to him, respectfully, as Mr. Blanco.

Mr. Blanco raised his eyes to the ceiling and shook his head, but what came out of his lips was a humble "I'm sorry, sweetheart."

The boys smiled at this spousal interaction.

Natalia continued, "It's important that you boys know what is happening in our country."

"You may not be aware of what is taking place," Mr. Blanco said, "because your parents wouldn't tell you, and—"

Natalia finished his thought: "Because your parents couldn't tell you. They were afraid of the committee and the spies. The committee is always listening."

One of the boys shouted, "You can't trust anybody!"

Another one interposed, "Anybody can be a spy."

And still another: "Yeah! Anything you say can get you into trouble."

"As my wife said," Mr. Blanco added, "it's important that you know the history. I don't want to forget any details, so I'm going to read to you from this newspaper article." He stood and pulled a newspaper page from his back pocket. Then he sat down again to read.

"This is what's written here: *In December 1961, Fidel Castro declared himself a Marxist Leninist. He went on to proclaim that Cuba was now an ally of the Soviet Union and an enemy of the United States. In addition, he began confiscating businesses, properties, and bank accounts in the name of the people—in other words, the Communist state.*"

Mr. Blanco regarded us. "Sounds familiar?"

"It sure does," one of the boys declared. "We lost everything."

"They took away our house and all the money we had in the bank," another one shouted.

One of the boys got teary eyed. "They stole all of our possessions. Everything."

"Yes, everyone here has lost much," Natalia said sympathetically. She turned to her husband. "Continue reading, Lorenzo."

Mr. Blanco read. "*Churches, houses of worship, and the clergy are attacked. Fidel Castro has also confiscated private schools and mandated that schools teach Communism and atheism. God is dead. There is no God. A* rumor ran among families that caused panic: Castro was sending children to the Soviet Union for Communist indoctrination and to serve in work camps." He asked us, "Were you aware of that?"

"Yes," one of the boys volunteered, "that's what my parents were afraid of."

Natalia added, "Such was the beginning of the . . . How should I put it?" She thought for a moment. "Ah, the exodus of the refugee children—*your* exodus—to the United States." She observed us. "Any questions?"

Alex raised his hand and asked, "How long are we going to be here?"

"That's a good question," responded Mr. Blanco. "To be perfectly honest, we don't know for sure. What we do know is that this camp serves as a temporary accommodation. You will all be relocated to a more permanent place in due time—"

Again, Natalia finished his thoughts: "With a foster family, or a special school, or an orphanage."

One of the boys asked, "When will we see our families again?"

"I wish I could answer that question, I really do," said Mr. Blanco. "The truth is that this political situation is out of our control."

"But there is hope." Natalia turned to her husband. "Continue reading, honey."

"Yes, of course," Mr. Blanco said. "Listen to this, boys. *President Eisenhower's administration provides funds to support the children once they arrive in Miami.* Well, as you know, Kennedy is the president of the United States now. But to continue: *Father Bryan Walsh*— Father Walsh is a priest, and he's in charge of the Catholic Welfare Bureau. *Father Bryan Walsh met secretly with James Baker, the headmaster of an American school in Havana, to help parents exile their children.*"

"Give me a chance to read, honey." Natalia snatched the article from her husband's hand. "It says here, *Information spreads in secrecy throughout Cuba by way of underground organizations.*" She stopped reading and exclaimed, "I didn't know that!" She glanced at the article again. "*Communication among Cuban and American contacts is held at a minimum. To expedite the process . . .*" She trailed off and then whispered, "I think that was last year."

She glanced at the article again and continued reading. "*To expedite the process, the State Department of the United States announced a 'visa waiver' policy.*"

She perused the boys sitting in front of her. "Do you know what a visa waiver is?"

We all shrugged and looked at each other with blank expressions.

Mr. Blanco retrieved the newspaper article from his wife. "It means this: *Minors no longer need a visa to travel to the United States,*" he finished.

"And lo and behold," Natalia exclaimed, "*you* are here!" She gestured to all of us.

Mr. Blanco asked, "Any questions?"

We sat in silence, not knowing what to ask.

"Just know that we will do whatever we can to help you," Natalia added.

We looked at each other somberly, some of us staring silently into space as if we had been hypnotized.

"Having said that," Mr. Blanco said, "I think that you boys deserve another field trip."

"We'll plan something special and get back to you," Natalia promised. Our foster parents always tried their best to keep us occupied.

◉ ◉ ◉

SPRING TRAINING

One day soon after, Mr. Blanco and his wife gathered us in the living room. "We know that you boys love to go on field trips," Mr. Blanco began with a wide smile.

When he didn't get much of a reaction, he scrutinized the room.

"Well, am I right or what?"

Once prompted, everyone shouted their agreement.

"Do you boys keep up with the major leagues?"

"The major leagues?" one of the boys asked.

"Of course we do," said another one. "I think. What's that?"

"Baseball!" Mr. Blanco cried out. "You certainly must have heard of the New York Yankees, haven't you?" He scanned the room for feedback but didn't get any.

"The Yankees just happen to be the best team in the major leagues. They are the greatest ever, for crying out loud! Why, they won the World Series last year. They win it every year!"

We regarded each other uncertainly, not understanding Mr. Blanco's zeal.

"Well, how would you boys like to go to a Yankees baseball game?"

"Yeah, okay," one boy stated, not quite wholeheartedly.

"We have tickets!" Natalia exclaimed, trying to lift our spirits.

Regardless of our lack of enthusiasm, they took us to a spring exhibition game.

The bus ride took nearly two hours. If my memory serves, the New York Yankees were playing the Saint Louis Cardinals. I remember particularly liking the Cardinals' uniform. During the bus trip, Mr. Blanco kept reminding us that the Yankees were the best team in baseball. He was certainly more excited about this field trip than we were.

Alex and I sat together in the stadium. "Did you ever watch a baseball game?" he asked.

"No. Did you?"

"My dad took me to a game once, but I don't remember anything about it. I think Cienfuegos was playing because that was his favorite team. They were called *los Elefantes* [the Elephants]."

"They wore green caps," I recalled from what one of my uncles had told me, "and their uniform had a lot of green in it."

"How about you?" Alex wanted to know. "Did you have a favorite team?"

"I liked Almendares, but I have no idea why. Well, because my family liked them. Their cap was blue. I don't know why, but I remember colors. Their uniform had a lot of blue in it. My uncle told me that Almendares was one of the oldest and most respected of the Cuban teams."

"What do you know about American teams?"

"Nothing," I answered. "I don't know much about baseball, really. Do you?"

"Nah."

I did develop an interest in baseball a couple of years later. It's a shame that on this particular field trip I might have seen such Yankee greats as Mickey Mantle, Yogi Berra, and Roger Maris but not appreciated the significance. Maris was coming off a most valuable player award after hitting sixty-one home runs, setting a season record. Mickey Mantle hit fifty-four home runs for a close second.

It is also quite possible that Stan Musial, one of the most illustrious Cardinals ever to play the game, played on that day—as well as such Cardinal greats as Bob Gibson and Ken Boyer. But how would I ever know?

What is the expression? If a tree falls in the forest and there's nobody around to hear, does it make a sound? Well, if I saw baseball royalty but wasn't aware of it, did I really see baseball royalty? It's a philosophical question that makes you wonder.

At least I appreciated the Cardinals' uniform.

"Look at how great they look!" I pointed. "There's a yellow bat on the shirt with two red birds on it."

"Those are cardinals," Alex said as if I were slow on the uptake. "That's why that team is called the Cardinals."

"Gee," I teased him, "you're so funny!"

I can't remember anything about the game, except that the players kept hitting very high pop flies.

"Wow!" exclaimed Alex, pointing to a high pop-up. "Look at that ball!"

I agreed. "I've never seen a ball hit that high!"

"It just keeps climbing up and up!" a boy shouted.

"It's going to the moon!" another cried out.

Who won the game? It didn't matter; it was just an exhibition game. Besides, I can't confirm that the Yankees actually played the Cardinals on that very day. It's possible that I got that game mixed up with another one.

◉ ◉ ◉

THEY BEAT YOU UP!

The camp was home to boys under the age of thirteen and girls up to the age of nineteen. Years later I learned that thirteen-year-old boys and older were sent to another camp. The prevailing wisdom at the time was that once a boy turns thirteen, he begins to notice girls. Thus, the genders had to be kept away from each other.

One day, a bunch of us, boys and girls, including some of the older girls, congregated on the sidewalk outside one of the houses, discussing our futures.

"You know this place is temporary," said one of the older girls. "Don't you?"

"What do you mean?" asked one of the younger boys.

"We won't be here forever," she answered. "They're going to send us either to a foster home or to an orphanage."

"Pray that they send you to a foster home," said another one of the big girls.

The views of the big girls held a lot of weight.

"Yeah," said another, "you don't want to go to an orphanage."

"Why not?" asked Norma, concerned.

"Because they beat you up," said one of the boys, "that's why!"

"No, they don't!" I refuted the boy's statement—not so much because this was my belief but because I didn't want Norma to be frightened.

"They do so!" the boy insisted.

"That's right," said another boy, calmly. "That's what they do."

"And they whip you," alleged one of the big girls. She was chewing bubble gum.

"Thirty lashes," another boy added.

"Get outta here!" hollered Alex. "I don't believe it."

"Neither do I," said another boy.

The oldest girl addressed that boy and Alex. "Neither one of you has any idea what you are talking about." She proceeded to confirm the alarming story. "I know for a fact that they beat you up!"

"And they whip you!" repeated the gum-chewing girl as she blew a large bubble.

"Thirty lashes," reiterated the oldest girl.

Norma looked upset, so I blurted out, "This is ridiculous. All it does is scare us all half to death. It solves nothing!" I turned to my sister. "Come on, Norma, let's get out of here."

I took my sister by the hand. As we were leaving, the girl who started the conversation yelled at us, "You can choose not to believe it, but that doesn't mean it ain't so!"

When we were a safe distance away, I held Norma by the shoulders. "I promise, Norma, that I will never leave you. I will always protect you!"

Norma smiled weakly and embraced me.

◉ ◉ ◉

THE CRUISE

One day, our foster parents told us that we were going on a cruise. As opposed to the Yankees' game, this announcement was met with raucous affirmation.

"It'll take about two and a half hours," Mr. Blanco said.

"We'll circle Miami Beach," Natalia added.

"But don't you worry, boys," Mr. Blanco assured us. "We'll have plenty to eat, and there'll be lots of soda pop to drink."

"When do we leave?" I asked.

"Tomorrow morning."

We woke up early the following morning. A bus took us to the pier, where a very large party boat was waiting for us. We were all excited as we boarded the vessel. A familiar song poured from its sound system.

"'Volaré'!" exclaimed Alex. "I love that song."

"Me too. It was so popular back home."

The pilot's voice interrupted the song. "It's a beautiful, sunny day. We'll be cruising around Miami Beach."

Alex and I joined some of our friends on deck. After fifteen or twenty minutes, a man in a sailor's uniform emerged from a cabin.

"Do you see that boat down yonder?" He pointed to a spot in the distance. "We are going aboard that son of a gun."

As that boat approached ours, Caridad, Norma's foster mother, materialized and said, "Get ready to enter that thing."

Norma joined me, and I looked at her in amazement. "Norma! Where did you come from? And your foster mother?"

"What do you mean?" she asked. "We've been here all along."

The other boat approached, and we proceeded to enter it, Caridad cautioning us, "Steady now; it can be rocky."

The day suddenly grew foggy. As the first boat sailed away, it disappeared.

A figure exited from another cabin and approached us. At first, neither Norma nor I could perceive who that person was. Slowly, our eyes focused through the fog, and we ascertained that it was our mother.

"Mom!" I cried out. "How did you get here?"

"Stop asking questions," ordered the sailor. "Go hug her!"

As the three of us embraced, the skies darkened. Almost immediately, thunder and lightning filled the heavens.

"It's a tempest!" yelled the sailor.

Without any warning, the waves started rocking our boat. The waves grew in intensity and sprayed the vessel with water. The boat swayed left and right. A very large wave—a *huge* wave—abruptly rose high above, ominously hovered over us for what seemed like an eternity, and crashed down onto the ocean craft. Water gushed in from both sides.

An even higher wave climbed into the heavens, and just like the other one, it suspended itself for a moment, then promptly collapsed onto the craft with such tremendous force that water flooded the port side. The boat teetered sideways momentarily, ever so slowly sinking into the menacing ocean waters.

Until it finally capsized.

We were thrown into the sea. Scary shark fins circled us.

"Mom! Norma!" I shouted, frantically trying to stay afloat. "Where are you?"

The night turned pitch black. I could not locate my loved ones. Through the darkness I discerned a fin moving rapidly towards me. A gigantic shark ascended from the water and opened its massive mouth, showing its rotating, swordlike teeth. I flailed my arms in desperation. Those lethal daggers were about to pierce right through my skin!

"*¡Auxilio! ¡Socorro!*" (Help! Help!) I yelled, panic stricken.

I suddenly heard a soft voice. "Are you okay, Tony?"

A worried Alex was shaking me so vigorously that I nearly fell off the top bunk. I sat up in bed in a cold sweat, trembling, perspiration flowing down my face. *It's a dream. Thank God it's just a dream!*

I steadied myself and answered, whispering so as not to arouse the others, "Yeah. I'm okay, Alex. It's just a nightmare. I'm sorry that I woke you up. Go back to sleep."

"Nah," he replied. "I don't sleep anymore. I just lie awake in bed all night, thinking of Cuba."

The nightmare underscored my trepidation about what was in store for us.

A few days later, we received a proclamation concerning our future.

◉ ◉ ◉

INDIANA

As we entered her office, the lady with the large glasses greeted us with a clipboard. "We have great news!" she proclaimed. "We have found a special place for you, a really nice place. You said that you want to go to"—she looked at the clipboard—"a place where it snows all the time." Smiling broadly, she strode to a map of the United States on the wall. "Come, let me show you."

We sauntered over to the wall. She placed her index finger on a spot on the map. "This is Indiana, your new home."

"Indiana?" My sister rubbed her forehead. "Is that where the Indians live?"

"That's just the name of the state."

"State?" I asked. "You mean, like, a state of . . . confusion?"

"It's like this," the lady tried to explain. "In Cuba you have provinces. In the United States you have states. I thought I had mentioned this before. Anyway, that's why they call it the United *States*."

"And it snows all the time there?" I asked.

"Yes, of course! Well, except that—"

I interrupted her. "Is it snowing there now?"

"No, not right now. That's what I'm trying to tell you. It snows in the winter."

"And this is not winter?"

"It is not." She motioned with her head to a calendar on the wall. "Today is the second of May. It's springtime."

"So, it is not snowing there now."

"Like I just said"—she sounded a little annoyed—"it's springtime. It snows in the winter." She sighed at my confused expression. "You're not familiar with the four seasons, are you? Of course not; you're from the tropics. Let me show you." She gestured to the map. "Come, let's take another look."

We moved a little closer to the map. "This is Indiana." She showed us again where Indiana was located and moved her hand to a place far below it. "Here's Miami. That's where the airport is." She positioned her index finger a few miles south of Miami. "Unfortunately, Florida City is not shown on this map, but that's where we are right now. In order to give you a little perspective, Florida City is about thirty-five miles south of Miami, and as I just mentioned, the airport is in Miami."

"Is thirty-five miles far?" I had no idea what that distance meant.

"By bus, mmm, it's about thirty to forty, maybe forty-five minutes, depending on traffic, of course."

I scratched my head, trying to comprehend what she was telling us.

Seeing my uncertainty, she tried to clarify. "It's about how long a lesson in class takes."

"Oh! Okay." I still was unsure about what forty-five minutes meant.

My sister inquired, "And we're going to another camp there?"

"Yes! Well, no. You're going to an orphanage. Saint Vincent's Orphanage."

"Orphanage!" My sister was terrified.

"We were hoping for a foster home," I said.

"Oh, but Saint Vincent's Orphanage is a really nice place!"

Norma was adamant. "We don't want to go to an orphanage!"

"Why not? What's wrong with an orphanage?"

"They beat you up!"

"That's not true," the lady insisted.

"They even whip you!" Norma got teary eyed.

"What? Who told you that?"

"That's what we heard!" Norma broke down sobbing. The lady with the large glasses was moved to embrace her.

"That's not true at all, honey! Who told you that?"

"It's true, ma'am," I conveyed to the lady. "That's what all the kids are saying."

The lady inhaled deeply and exhaled. She proceeded to two holy portraits hanging on the wall—one of the Sacred Heart of Jesus and the other of the Virgin Mary.

Then she brought out the heavy artillery.

"I swear," she said as she placed her hand over her heart, then pointed to the first portrait, "by the blood of the Sacred Heart of Jesus"—she made the sign of the cross and pointed to the second portrait—"and His Blessed Mother"—she made a cross with her thumb and index finger and kissed them—"that you have *nothing* to fear!" Her gaze burned into our eyes. "Norma Eulalia, Juan Antonio, you have *nothing* to fear."

I thought, *Wow! The lady with the large glasses swore in the name of God and the Virgin Mary!* What could I say?

Norma smiled weakly and nodded. She was sold. The only response I could think of was to ask, "When do we leave?"

"Tomorrow morning."

◎ ◎ ◎

ANOTHER GOODBYE

It was quite early and still dark. A bus waited for us by the gate. A few children also waited there. I thought of Alex. He had left the camp a few days earlier. Once again, we only found out about someone's departure by their absence in the morning. *Where did they take him?* I wondered. *Is he in an orphanage, or in a foster home, or with his mom and dad?*

Mr. Blanco brought me back to reality as he climbed into his car after dropping Norma and me off. He waved at us. "I have to go now and look after my other boys. Have a safe trip!"

"Thank you, sir, for all you've done." I waved back as his car sped away.

A couple of nuns stood beside the lady with the large glasses. She held her clipboard and started calling each child by name.

Most of the children had already been called when our turn finally came. The lady looked at us. "Norma Eulalia, Juan Antonio, you may enter the bus now."

My sister ran to the lady with the large glasses to give her a hug, wrapping her arms around the lady's waist as she had done before. Visibly affected, the lady crouched down and cuddled Norma affectionately.

She turned to me and winked. "I promise you that you're going to a very nice place." She beheld Norma's eyes and vowed, "*They* are very nice people, and I promise, one more time, *they* are going to take good care of you."

As she had the previous day, Norma smiled weakly and nodded.

I expressed my appreciation and extended my hand. "We are very grateful to you for all you've done for us."

Shaking my hand, she said, "You have no idea what your words mean to me. Let me tell you truthfully, it has been my pleasure to be of service to you." She kissed me on the left cheek and likewise kissed Norma on hers.

Then we climbed onto the bus.

When all the children had entered, the nuns waved at us. One of them said, "Have a safe flight!"

The door closed, and off we went to the airport.

◉ ◉ ◉

Reflecting on our stay at the Florida City camp, I have to admit that a very important feature we lacked there was *structure*. This is quite understandable given the circumstances. No one ever expected so many children to arrive from Cuba within a period of twenty-two months. As best as I can recollect, an effort was made to offer academic instruction, though I don't remember attending formal classes. We were pretty much free to come and go as we pleased—within the confines of our little community, of course; after all, we were fenced in.

To their credit, our foster parents attempted to bring some kind of routine to our days, such as scheduling mealtimes. But this was a difficult task given that the dining hall was always open. Many children took consolation in food—pretty much as an alcoholic does with liquor—by frequenting the dining hall as often as they liked, often pampering themselves by consuming an extra meal a day.

Sad to say, Norma and I were not exempt from this practice. Many of the children there, including the two of us, put on weight. Two especially tempting treats also contributed to this: the soda machines and the ice cream truck. This was how we spent most of our weekly allowance. I can't remember if it was fifty cents or one dollar, but it was more than enough to satisfy our daily whims. It only cost ten cents for a large glass bottle of soda. My flavor of choice was orange, but I could not, for the life of me, like root beer. My favorite treat from the ice cream truck was a banana split sundae, which came in an elliptical bowl with three very generous scoops of ice cream (vanilla, chocolate, and strawberry), each with a cherry on top. The whole thing was covered with fudge and sprinkles, topped off with a little umbrella or a plastic American flag in the center.

In retrospect, our foster parents should have stepped in and limited this unhealthy gratification, but they didn't. I suspect, out of some misguided affection, they preferred to allow us to indulge rather than deprive us of this pleasure.

Such a practice would not continue at Saint Vincent's Orphanage. Thank goodness!

PART TWO

Journey into the Unknown

In you, Lord, I take refuge...
For you are my rock and my fortress

Psalm 31:2–4

CHAPTER V

Saint Vincent's Orphanage

The plane ride—or rather, the plane *rides*—to Indiana took all day. We made several stops along the way in order to hook up with various connecting flights. As soon as we landed at an airport, we had to get off that plane and board another one. The process was repeated four or five, maybe even six times. Motion sickness was the prevailing theme, and we made use of the brown paper bag numerous times.

This was a great way to lose some weight, although I don't recommend it.

It was nightfall when we finally arrived at our destination: Evansville, Indiana. A bus was waiting at the airport, and a man wearing black clerical clothes with a white collar greeted us.

"Welcome to Indiana!" he hailed. "I'm Father So-and-So, and I'm going to drive you to Saint Vincent's Orphanage." I don't remember his name, though he became a staple of my time at the orphanage. By the same token, I have no idea how he really greeted us because I didn't speak a word of English at the time. I surmise that this is what Father So-and-So must have said.

I have no memory whatsoever of that trip to Saint Vincent's, except that it probably took more than an hour and it was pitch black by the time we arrived at the front entrance of the orphanage. Norma and I must have fallen asleep. We had departed Florida City in the dark of dawn and arrived in Indiana in the dark of night.

As at the camp in Florida City, the nuns waiting for us wore long, black habits, but with smaller white veils. About a dozen children, maybe more, got off the bus.

We were led into a very large refectory with four long rows of tables.

Each table had six chairs, and each table had been set for a meal. One set of rows was for the girls, the other for the boys. We were asked to stand by our table as a nun addressed us.

Later we learned that this was Mother Superior. As with Father So-and-So, I have no idea what she said. This is how it sounded to me: "*Welcometosaintvincentsorphanageweareverypleasedtohaveyouasournew residents.*"

We made the sign of the cross: "In the name of the Father, and of the Son, and of the Holy Ghost. Amen." In those days we said, "Holy Ghost." Nowadays we say, "Holy Spirit."

Mother Superior then guided us in prayer. "Bless us, O Lord, and these Thy gifts, which we are about to receive from Thy bounty, through Christ, our Lord. Amen." We made the sign of the cross again and took our seats. Every meal was preceded and followed by the sign of the cross. Of course, the Cuban children could not follow along since we did not speak English, but since this is the prayer we always invoked before each meal and eventually I could understand it, it is a very safe assumption that this is the one that was said.

The nuns served us our supper. At the orphanage we would have breakfast, dinner, and supper—not breakfast, lunch, and dinner. The term *lunch* was never mentioned there. As with all of our suppers, this one was probably rather simple. I don't recall what kind of meat we had, if any, since it was late. It was probably chicken. But maybe we just had cold cuts.

Regular meals, for the most part, consisted of green beans, which was our mainstay vegetable, along with sliced white bread, a potato of some kind—either baked, boiled, broiled, or mashed—and a new kind of green vegetable which was ever present. They called it celery. Yuk! It took me some time to get used to it because I found it completely devoid of taste. But I discovered that if I sprinkled a little salt on it and smothered it with mayonnaise, it became somewhat palatable—but I must underscore the word *somewhat*.

For dessert we probably had ice cream on a stick or some kind of cream pie. Such desserts were specialties reserved for Sundays, holidays, and other special days, and today was a special day indeed.

As I mentioned before, my memory is much better than Norma's. She remembers practically nothing of Cuba and very little of either the camp at Florida City or Saint Vincent's Orphanage. However, she maintains that on Sundays the meals at Saint Vincent's were special. Norma contends that at dinnertime we were served all the chili we could eat. In addition, Norma claims that on Sunday evenings we were served pizza and something that resembled a grilled cheese sandwich. Basically, it was white bread with American cheese melted on top.

I don't recall ever having such meals. In fact, the first pizza I remember having was about a year later in New York. Notwithstanding, Norma asserts that this is the way it was.

I must admit, I have no alternative memory. Therefore, that's the way it was.

◉ ◉ ◉

JUST ANTONIO

After that first supper, we were interviewed individually. One of the nuns guided me into a small room. She glanced at my name on a sheet of paper and struggled with the pronunciation. "Your name is *Joo*-Ann Ann-*toe*-nee-owe *Dough*-rah, and your last name is *Try*-vee-aye-sew. Is that right? Tell me your full name. By the way, we're very happy to have you here at Saint Vincent's Orphanage."

Well, maybe that's what she said. Remember, I didn't speak a word of English. She pointed to a blank sheet of paper. *Is she asking me to write my name?* I wrote it down and recited it out loud: "Juan Antonio Dora Travieso"—too quickly, perhaps, because she stared at me apprehensively, as if I had the proverbial two heads on my shoulders.

In Spanish-speaking countries, both the paternal and maternal surnames are used. The paternal surname goes before the maternal one. I was not aware that in the United States the maternal one is not used—in my case, Travieso. I wonder if she herself was aware of this difference.

I repeated my full name a little bit slower: "Juan Antonio Dora Travieso."

I was still going too fast for her. "*Joo*-Ann," she said, emphasizing the first syllable.

"No," I corrected her, accentuating the second syllable and correct pronunciation, "Hoo-*ahn*." She looked at me dubiously. I reiterated it slowly, making sure to put the stress on the last syllable: "Juan."

She stared at me, befuddled. "Won!" *Is that really what she thought I said?*

I stated it once more, this time slower: "Hoooo-*aaahnnn*." And at a normal pace: "Juan."

She looked at me quizzically and raised her index finger. "One?" I could tell that she was really baffled.

"No. Hoooo-*aaahnnn*. Juan."

She shook her head and pointed to the paper. She changed tactics and tried saying my middle name, very slowly, at a snail's pace. "Ann-*toe-nee-owe?*"

"Yes!" I said in English, trying to impress her with my linguistic skills, except that it came out sounding like "Jess!"

"Good!" she exclaimed.

Success at last! She seemed to gain her confidence and tried her luck with my maternal surname. "*Try*-vee-aye-sew?"

She was really struggling with this.

"Jess!" I gave her the benefit of the doubt, overlooking the fact that the correct emphasis was on the third syllable and not the first one.

"Tony es mi apodo." I tried to explain to her that Tony was my nickname. "Ah-*poh*-doh."

"Ah-poe-*dough?*" *Oh no! I confused her!*

I attempted to clarify that the emphasis was on the middle syllable: "Ah-*poh*-do."

"Ah-*poe*-dough?"

Why did I have to bring up my nickname? I reprimanded myself.

I shrugged and said, "Okay." After all, she did put the accent on the second syllable.

She shook her head. "No, not Ah-*poe*-dough." She directed her attention to my last names on the sheet of paper. "*Dough*-rah *Try*-vee-aye-sew."

Boy, this was getting tough! I enunciated my maternal last name, with the emphasis on the third syllable: "Trah-vee-*eh*-saw."

"Try-vee-aye-*sew*?" Now she put the emphasis on the last syllable.

"No." I said it slowly: "Travieso."

"Try . . . vee . . . *eh* . . . saw."

"Jess! Travieso!" She finally got the emphasis on the third syllable; we were getting somewhere!

But she didn't think so. "No, no, no!" She shook her head again and flailed her arms in exasperation. "Not Try-vee-*aye*-sew! Not Ah-*poe*-dough! Not *Joo*-Ann! Just . . ." She covered her face with her hands. "Just Ann-*toe*-nee-owe!" She took a long breath. "Okay? Antonio Dora! Period!"

And that's how I became just Antonio Dora. Short, simple, and to the point. I sort of liked the simplification of my name.

And everyone called me Antonio. Period!

◉ ◉ ◉

VINCENNES

Saint Vincent's Orphanage was located in a farming community in Vincennes, Indiana. You could tell who the locals were by the way they pronounced the name of the town: "*Vihn*-sense"—emphasizing the first syllable. Everyone else struggled with the pronunciation. Named after a town in France, its actual pronunciation would sound something like "Vahn-*sehnn*."

Vincennes was founded in 1732 by French fur traders and is located in the southwestern part of the state, about 130 miles south of the capital,

Indianapolis, and 55 miles or so north of Evansville. We rarely ventured beyond the orphanage walls. From time to time, the nuns would take us out for a walk along dirt roads, but not far from the orphanage. Sometimes a tractor, a truck, or a car drove by. We would wave at the drivers, and they would wave back at us, smiling.

For some of the older boys, temptation lurked beyond the perimeters of the orphanage grounds—a watermelon patch! It belonged to a farmer. One day, a few ventured out and stole some watermelons. Well, they did not take the watermelons with them. Instead, they would pick up a watermelon and let it fall on the ground so that it cracked open, and then help themselves to the fruit. They cracked open quite a number of watermelons in this fashion.

The next day, the infuriated farmer paid a visit to the orphanage and complained to Mother Superior that her boys were stealing his watermelons.

"Cubans!" A boy named Wyatt always blamed the Cubans whenever anything went wrong; so did Favian, his younger brother, their friend Marshall, and some of the other boys. Wyatt was a bully, and he was always picking on the little kids.

As it turned out, the watermelon caper was not the Cubans' fault, and the nuns instinctively knew who the guilty were. Those boys were confronted. They confessed and were punished, though their names and how they were punished was kept between the nuns and the culpable group. But the attempts at discretion really didn't matter. Those boys were fearless and continued to pursue their delinquent ways, so their identities were no secret.

For his part, Wyatt kept on blaming the Cubans whenever anything went wrong.

At first, neither Favian nor Marshall nor some of the other native English speakers thought very highly of the Cubans, and vice versa. It's not like we fought each other. We just looked at each other askance. In fact, we tried not to make eye contact. Simply put, neither group was quite sure what to make of the strangers in their midst. The issue came down to, I think, our inability to communicate with each other. After all, the Americans and the Canadians had no idea who we were and why we were coming to Saint Vincent's Orphanage in droves. To them, we were just outsiders invading their territory. Once the Cubans learned to speak English, both groups' outlooks began to change.

Favian had a lot of maturing to do in order to accept us. And Marshall and the others took their cue from him. In the long run, Favian and Marshall's perceptions of the new arrivals changed, while Wyatt remained pretty much the same—a nasty and angry guy.

It took a bit of maturation for the Cubans to accept the residents as well. Eventually, Favian, Marshall, and I became good friends—with emphasis on the word *eventually*. Favian was the star of the basketball team and, in my opinion, a born athlete. He was also one of the nicest kids around, constantly apologizing for his older brother's behavior. Marshall turned out to be one of the funniest kids I've met in my whole life, even to this day. He was a very good basketball player too.

◉ ◉ ◉

LONDRI

Julián Londres was my best friend. We hit it off from the start. He had a great sense of humor. "They call me Laundry," he explained to me, "because they couldn't pronounce my last name, Londres." *Londres* is the Spanish name for London, the capital of England.

"What's wrong with Londres? It's not a difficult name."

"Not for you and me, perhaps. Just think how hard we find English pronunciation."

When I tried to say "Laundry," it came out sounding like "*Lohn-dree*." If you spell that sound in Spanish, it would be "Londri." So, that's what I called him.

We Cubans often gathered together in the playground to discuss our new reality. A day comes to mind when we were discussing our relationship with the English-speaking natives who lived among us. Londri proposed that we should not view them in a negative way.

"They are not the enemy. Why look at them in such a fashion?"

"That's true," I agreed. "They are not the enemy."

"Always remember that Fidel Castro is the one and only enemy," Londri reminded us. "Never forget that. It is because of that tyrant that we are in this place."

"I have an idea," one of the Cuban boys offered. "When you run into one of them, smile."

"That's a great idea!" I added. Londri and I took turns shaking hands with that boy. A few of the kids appeared a little doubtful. The majority, however, nodded in agreement. I could sense that our outlook was beginning to change for the better.

◉ ◉ ◉

In the meantime, I found time to write our mother another letter:

Hi, Mom,

How are you? I am fine. Me and Norma are in an orphanage now. The address is: Saint Vincent's Orphanage, RR 4, Vincennes, Indiana.

The kids here say that RR stands for railroad, so there must be a railroad somewhere here in this town. There are hundreds of kids here! We have six dormitories. I am in D6 and Norma is in D4. We do everything here. We eat and play here, and we go to school here. We go to Mass every day and pray in the chapel before supper. I'm an altar boy. They are really nice people, and they are taking very good care of us, just like you told us. Well, write soon and tell us when you are coming.

Your son Tony and your daughter Norma.

PS: They call me Antonio.

I later discovered that RR didn't stand for *railroad* but for *rural route*. Mom sent us a reply; following is a shortened version of her letter:

> *Darling son and daughter:*
> *I'm so glad that you are well. Tony, it's so nice that they call you Antonio. Now we have another reason for writing RASA ["Reservado a San Antonio"] on the back of envelopes. Nothing much has changed here, except that I'm making every effort to join you as soon as possible. God willing, that day will soon be upon us. You can count on that. Tony, look after Normita. Normita, respect Tony. He is your father substitute.*
>
> *These are trying times. Pray to God to grant us the fortitude to carry on through this dark period. Remember these verses from the twenty-third Psalm:*
> *The Lord is my shepherd; there is nothing I lack.*
> *Even though I walk through the valley of the shadow of death, I will fear no evil, for God is always with me.*
>
> *Love and kisses,*
Mom

◉ ◉ ◉

STRUCTURE

Saint Vincent's Orphanage ran under a tight schedule. Each day was structured. We went to Mass in the morning, had breakfast, completed our chores, and went to class. We had recess, ate dinner, and went to the playground. We returned to the classroom for three hours, back to the playground, then chapel for evening prayers before supper. On Sundays we wore what was called our "Sunday best" when we went to church and breakfast afterwards. The boys wore black shoes, dark-colored slacks, and dress shirts in subdued pastel colors—soft yellow, green, or blue, with the top button fastened. The girls wore skirts with a white blouse and black shoes with white bobby socks. In church the girls wore doily lace caps. Both genders wore sports jackets in winter.

As opposed to the Florida City camp, we had no nighttime snacks. Supper was our last meal of the day. Thank goodness! This was a better and healthier practice. We also did not receive an allowance. The only time we were allocated any money was during a couple of field trips.

When we went back to the classroom in the evening, we did our homework and received additional support. We read children's magazines and learned how to darn our socks and stitch torn shirts. We even learned how to sew small, leather purses. Then we went to the recreation room, where we played cards and board games and read comic books. We watched TV at night, went to bed by nine or ten o'clock, and got up at six in the morning.

We even found time for what the nuns called spring cleaning chores: polishing and varnishing wood wherever it could be found, whether in bookcases, on tables and chairs, or especially the staircase railings.

It was quite a sight to behold—an army of children busily polishing and varnishing wood. How in heaven's name did we find time to do all of these things? Or better yet, how did the nuns do it? The nuns worked twenty-four-seven. They had shifts, so we always had a nun supervising us. They cooked for us and fed us, washed our clothes and dirty linen, nursed us when we were sick, prayed with us, and played with us. At night, while we were sleeping, a nun would walk the rows of beds with a flashlight to make sure everything was okay and, I suspect, to make sure that no one was up to any shenanigans.

They also disciplined us, and they taught us—teaching three grades in one classroom with sixty to seventy kids in one room. How did they do it? In one word: discipline. Another word: structure. That's what Saint Vincent's Orphanage offered that the Florida City camp did not.

I don't mean to diminish the contribution the Florida City camp made. At least the camps provided shelter, food, clothing, and—not least of all—hope. The camps recognized that they were a short-term safe haven as they sought to procure longer-lasting accommodations for the children.

As far as Saint Vincent's Orphanage is concerned, I honestly loved it there! Unfortunately, not everyone felt that way. Some of the girls, I suspect, would fall under this category. Did the nuns treat the boys better than they treated the girls? I really can't say for sure.

I can say that I once witnessed the nun in charge of D2, the younger boys' dormitory, slapping one of the youngsters under her care. While the rest of her boys were in line, walking back to their dormitory from the refectory, this little boy kept yelling and crying as the nun slapped him in the face over and over again. One of her favorite punishments for the boys she called "sissies" was to dress them up in girls' clothing and make them reside in the girls' dormitory for a few days. I remember one of these boys eating with the girls in the refectory while wearing a dress.

As far as I know, the nuns who inflicted corporal and psychological punishment were eventually removed from the orphanage. Furthermore, I researched the history of orphanages throughout the world and sadly discovered that, in some places, physical punishment was modus operandi, as the older children had insisted back at the camp in Florida. Charles Dickens wrote about the cruel treatment inflicted on children in his novel *Oliver Twist*. Truth be told, some Pedro Pan girls have revealed to me that they were mistreated in their respective orphanages.

All I can testify to is that the nuns I encountered were caring individuals. I believe that many of my dormitory mates would agree with me. To put things in perspective, some of the kids complained that they were forced to make their beds and carry out chores. At the same time, they admitted that their parents pampered them way too much. Cuban parents are notorious for spoiling their children. I was pampered myself, but I also appreciated, during my stay at Saint Vincent's Orphanage, that I was being taught essential tasks for everyday living—little things, such as minimal sewing, keeping an orderly locker, picking up after oneself, dusting, sweeping, and the like.

Furthermore, I was particularly fortunate to have been at Saint

Vincent's Orphanage during the era that preceded the Second Vatican Council, simply because of the workforce. We had lots of nuns.

After Vatican Two, which taught that salvation is offered to all, religious orders experienced quite a dip in the influx of young people interested in joining their congregations. The number of priests and nuns dwindled dramatically. Some felt the Vatican Two changes made their calling too mundane. Many left their parishes and congregations in order to get married and had to be replaced by laypeople. Up to this point, priests and nuns had been essentially working for free. Laypeople had to be paid. This had a profound influence on the orphanage, as well as schools, hospitals, parishes, and the various institutions within the Catholic Church.

◉ ◉ ◉

THE INTERIOR

There were six dormitories at Saint Vincent's orphanage, designated by a capital *D* for dormitory and a number. The babies were in D1. We had a few babies, but we seldom saw them. Those in grades one through three were in D2 for boys and D3 for girls. D4, my sister's dormitory, was for girls in grades four through six. D5 was for girls in grades seven and eight, while D6 was for boys from grades four through eight. I was in D6. We only had a handful of seventh and eighth-grade boys.

Most of the children at the orphanage were born in the United States, although a few were Canadian, but we never knew anyone's actual situation unless they themselves revealed it. Most of the children were truly orphaned. A small number came from difficult family situations: the parents were either in prison or had been deemed incompetent or negligent by courts of law. The Cuban children were different from the others in the sense that we were not orphaned. We were refugees—*political* refugees.

The D6 boys' sleeping quarters comprised an enormous chamber on the second floor with an extremely high ceiling. It was like a gigantic warehouse, with six or more rows of beds and about fifteen beds in each row and a wooden chair beside each bed. We laid our bathrobes on the chairs when we went to bed, and wore them for privacy as we were dressing or undressing.

The nuns taught us how to make our beds army-style; you could bounce a quarter off them. We were expected to make ours in a matter of minutes each morning as soon as we got up. As in an army, the nuns made a big deal about this to help us develop discipline and attention, even to the smallest details; that way we could concentrate on more important matters. We wondered if Mother Superior or Sister Kevin grew up in a military family.

Each of us had a locker, which we were expected to keep in orderly fashion. Frequent inspections were conducted to make sure that we kept our locker and our bed tidy. I took great pride in keeping the ones assigned to me in tip-top shape.

The rows of beds were spread along three walls with large windows in an inverted *U*. If you stood in front of the middle rear window, looking in the direction of the beds, you would see columns of lockers directly in front of the rows of beds, and off to the right was the group lavatory.

On entering the group lavatory, first you would see four or five columns of sinks; each column had four small sinks with a mirror. Beyond the sinks were the toilets. Neither the sinks nor the toilets had enclosures. There was no privacy here, but you soon got used to it. This arrangement became second nature.

Towards the rear, beyond the toilets, were the showers, maybe eight or ten of them. We wore our bathrobes and carried our towels and face cloths with us while we waited our turn to take a shower, but the wait was never long. We were taught to take care of our hygiene with military precision.

To enter a shower, we went past a curtain, the only hint of privacy we ever had in the group lavatory. No one could see us taking a shower.

We also had an indoor basketball court where we played during inclement weather. This was where the basketball team practiced before a game. It also served as an auditorium, which was where we played bingo, watched movies on a large screen, and were entertained by professional performers and in turn entertained the townsfolk with our theatrical holiday presentations, such as the Christmas show.

◉ ◉ ◉

CHORES

We were all assigned a daily chore as well as a weekly one. My weekly chore consisted of dusting the furniture in the recreation room. My daily chore was to sweep the first-floor hallway on weekdays and to wax it on Saturdays when we had no classes. It took about two or three hours to wax the hallway floor. On Sundays we had a day off. And, of course, the nuns inspected our work. I made a great effort to do a good job and took great pride in my labor.

Some of the older girls were assigned to the refectory, setting the tables before meals, serving the children, and cleaning up afterwards. We heard that the nuns were teaching some of them how to cook and prepare meals. Taking everything into account, these girls were getting practical experience should they ever need a job in a dining hall or restaurant.

Some of the kids complained that chores were tedious and monotonous. To make them fun, I made believe that I was competing in a major sport event, complete with fan participation. I was always playing for the championship. Naturally, I always won.

In my fancy, I could hear the fans cheering as I made the final shot at the buzzer to win a basketball tournament or hit a grand slam home run—with a full count and two outs in the bottom of the ninth inning—in the seventh game of the World Series. I would visualize my teammates hoisting me up and carrying me on their shoulders around the baseball park as the fans went wild.

I did not find the chores boring at all. As a matter of fact, I found them quite enjoyable and looked forward to doing them.

What can I say? I was a little weird.

◉ ◉ ◉

THE EXTERIOR

From the rear of our sleeping quarters as you looked out through the windows, you would see the great expanse of our playground. Your first point of reference was a huge water tower with the words *Saint Vincent School* scrawled on the tower itself. We could sit or stand or run about below the tower. To the left of the tower was a grassy area, and beyond that, down a short incline, a basketball court with a cement surface. Past the basketball court was a slope. To the left of the slope, about twenty yards away, were the swings. We also had monkey bars, seesaws, slides, and a merry-go-round.

We would run with wild abandon, jump rope, do cartwheels and backflips, and walk upright on our hands with our feet straight up in the air. We did all that, and more—effortlessly. I loved doing cartwheels and walking on my hands from the middle of the court to the landing, a distance of about five or six yards. Backflips looked a little too dangerous for my taste, especially over the cement ground of the basketball court. I was not the only one who felt that way, but a few of the kids were audacious, and a little cement ground wouldn't come between them and backflips. The older nuns would look at us and sigh, "Ah, youth!"

Why would they say that? I wondered. *What's the matter with them, anyway?* I believed that they could do these things if they only tried. *We do! It's so easy! All you have to do is run as fast as you can, jump, and throw yourself down on your hands. Your impulse would do the rest.*

I know now why the older nuns would sigh. These days I can barely bend down to pick something off the ground. Ah, middle age.

Well, let's call it maturity.

Beyond the basketball court slope, looking right about thirty yards away, were picnic tables outlined by trees and bushes stretching straight up the terrain into a forest. Conversely, if you stood in the middle of the basketball court, went down the slope, and walked straight, you would run into the baseball field. Beyond the baseball field was another slope—a steep decline that led to the aforementioned forest and, further on, the watermelon patch. We referred to this forest as "the jungle." The Cubans called it *la Casa del Diablo*—the Devil's House—but I have no idea why. Only a few brave souls frequented la Casa del Diablo. The name itself was daunting. I certainly was not one of the brave souls.

Every once in a while, one of the nuns would enter the playground carrying a very large, round, wooden basket full of apples, along with saltshakers. *Why the saltshakers?* I wondered. Marshall showed me why—not with words, but by eating those apples.

He would take a bite of an apple and sprinkle salt on it. He would then take another bite and sprinkle more salt on it, take a third bite, and so on. I had never seen anybody eat an apple that way. I mean the *entire* apple—skin, core, seeds and all!

"I just love apples!" Marshall exclaimed once.

"Really, Marshall? I wouldn't have guessed!" I replied.

◉ ◉ ◉

THE OTHER FIELD

There was a much larger baseball field, with bleachers, on another side of the orphanage grounds. We went there from time to time. It had a golf course where the townsfolk would tee off. Once, I remember hearing someone yelling, "Fore!" I didn't know what that meant; I thought it had to do with the number four. But why would anyone yell, "Four"? One of the boys told me that you were supposed to duck. I was confused. *Is he referring to the bird?* Then I spotted a man coming from the golf course, bleeding from the mouth. He walked right past me, nonchalantly. Apparently, his teeth got hit by a golf ball. For the life of me, I could not understand his casualness!

There were two big collies who were very friendly and loved to be petted, but what they really loved to do was chase cars. Whenever a car raced by, they ran after it. Those crazy dogs seemed to enjoy inhaling the fumes. Above all, however, they loved chasing rabbits. Once, one of the dogs caught a rabbit and, holding it in its mouth, paraded it around the grounds as if it were a trophy. We all applauded. If I am not mistaken, that dog actually acknowledged its audience, dropped its prize on the ground, and took a bow. It picked up its prize again and ran off into the woods.

What it did with the rabbit . . . ¡Yo qué sé! (I have no idea!)

CHAPTER VI

May

*Viewed freely, the English language
is the accretion and growth
of every dialect, race, and range of time,
and is both the free and compacted composition of all.*

Walt Whitman

Learning English became a priority, and we all put our hearts and souls into acquiring this new language replete with weird pronunciations and diphthongs.

The Pedro Pan children attended regular classes with the English-speaking kids. Even though this was prior to ESL (English as a Second Language), we had an advantage—we were surrounded by English twenty-four-seven. All we had to do was listen and try to duplicate the sounds we heard.

I do remember, however, having individual lessons in the beginning with Sister Kevin.

Sister Kevin was in charge of the D6 boys. The black habit could not hide her youth and attractiveness. She had a great sense of humor, but she suffered no fools. One thing you learned quickly was not to cross her. She did not hesitate to dispense discipline—if you deserved it.

One of her favorite punishments was to have us write a chain of one hundred words. This is how it worked: whatever word you chose, the last letter of that word would become the first letter of the next word. For example, if you wrote the word *fruit*, the next letter would begin with a *t*—such as *television* or *team* or *train*. Let's say that you chose *network*; the next word would begin with a *k*. From there you would go on building the chain—thus: *king, game, elephants, silver,* and so on.

The exercise did not help us learn the definition of the word, but it did help us develop vocabulary. Sister Kevin allowed us to use a dictionary, and there were a few small dictionaries in the rec room from which we could acquire the definition of the words we chose to write—should we bother, of course.

Sometimes, when a transgression had been committed by someone but the identity of that particular individual was unknown, Sister Kevin would just punish everyone. In such cases, we all had to write a chain of one hundred words. We would go to the rec room and assist each other in our search for words in the dictionaries. This bonding experience helped us make new friends. To tell you the truth, it didn't feel like punishment at all.

Sister Kevin likely saw the word chain as a learning opportunity. She always insisted on teaching us proper English; all of the nuns did, for that matter. And in spite of the occasional usage of phrases like *gonna, gotta, hafta, wanna,* and *ain't,* all of the kids spoke proper English. Thus, the Cubans learned proper English. We were not exposed to street slang—and certainly not to curse words.

As for tidbits about Sister Kevin, the gossipmongers said she grew up with five older brothers who taught her how to fight. They also spread a rumor that one of the big kids once struck her in the face with a sucker punch. She recovered quickly and swung right back and smacked the boy on the nose, and they went at it, toe to toe.

Needless to say, Sister Kevin won that fight. From that day on, no one dared cross her.

Anyway, that was the rumor.

At any rate, she was always fair, and I was truly fortunate to have her as our dormitory leader and teacher.

One of the first words she taught me was *scissors*—a very useful word, which I pronounced "*see*-sores." Sister Kevin would listen to my pronunciation and smile.

"Listen to me, Antonio," she would say. "Scissors. Sssci-sssors."

"*See*-sores."

There were times when she couldn't keep a straight face. "Okay, Antonio, we'll try again tomorrow. Don't worry; you will get it."

The word *girl* was likewise very difficult to articulate. When I first tried to say it, it came out sounding like "gggrrrolll."

"Antonio," Sister Kevin said, "you are a boy and your sister is a . . ."

To which I would reply, "Gggrrrolll."

"Listen to me: gggiiirrlll."

"Gggrrrolll."

"Okay, let's try this: you are a boy and your sister is . . ."

"Norma."

She laughed heartily. She had a great sense of humor. I loved this about her.

"Don't you worry, Antonio. You'll get it!"

"Jess!"

"We will tackle the word *yes* tomorrow, Antonio. Yes, we will. *Eeee-ehsss.*"

In those days prior to the Second Vatican Council, some of the nuns took a male name. Sister Kevin was one of them. The nuns usually chose the name of a saint, or the name of someone of historical or patriotic significance, or the name of a respected and esteemed family member. In many instances, the first name would be Mary, in honor of Our Blessed Mother—that is, the mother of Jesus—followed by a second name, whether it be a male name or not.

In this manner, Sister Kevin's full name would be Sister Mary Kevin.

After Vatican Two, many nuns assumed their own names. The vast majority wore either simplified habits or no habits at all. Makeup remained taboo. Eventually, a little subtle makeup was allowed.

☉ ☉ ☉

THE BIG Y

"Antonio, let's practice the sound of *y* in front of a word," Sister Kevin said to me during one of our individual lessons. "For example, the word *yes*. That word is a common and very useful word. Say 'yes.'"

"Jess."

"Antonio, just say, 'Eeeeh.'"

"Eeeeh."

"That's right. Now say, 'Ehsss.'"

"Ehsss."

"Now put it together: eeeh-ehsss."

"Eeeh-ehsss."

"Now say it quickly: 'eeehesss.'"

"Eeehess."

"Yes! Congratulations, mister, you just pronounced the word *yes*!"

"Yes!"

"Let's look at words that begin with the letter *y*." She leafed through a dictionary. "Ah, here's a whole bunch of words. Let's pick some common ones. How about *you*? Antonio, say, 'You.'"

"Jooh."

"Listen, Antonio: eeeh-oooh. Say it."

"Eeeh-oooh."

"Quickly."

"Eeeoooh . . . you."

"*You* said it, *young* man! Now say, 'Young.'"

"Johng."

"Eeeh-ohng."

"Eeeh-ohng."

"Quickly."

"Eeeohng. Young!"

"*You* said it, *young* man!"

"I am a young man."

"*Yes*! *You* are learning, kiddo!" She looked through the dictionary. "How about a color: *yellow*. Wait, say it slowly at first: eeeh . . ."

"Eeeh-eh-low. Yellow!"

"*You* are getting the hang of it. Remember to begin with eeeh."

We went through a whole list of words that began with the letter *y*—*year, your, yard, yesterday, York, Yankees, youthful.* At the end of the lesson, she said, "*You* have done it, *young* man. *You* are now able to say what *you* could not say *yesterday*. Congratulations!"

"Jess!"

◎ ◎ ◎

THE OTHER KIDS

Besides Londri, Favian also became one of my best friends. As I have mentioned before, he was affable, unpretentious, and he was the star of the basketball team. We had a very interesting team. We played twelve games and lost every one of them. However, there was a reason for that. Our squad had no eighth graders and only one or two seventh graders, and we were playing teams with eighth graders who towered way over us. I'll talk more about our team in subsequent chapters.

As I have also mentioned previously, Favian's older brother, Wyatt—a tall and lanky kid with a mean streak—loved to pick on me and the other little kids. He seldom smiled and always seemed angry. No two brothers could be more different!

We had three sets of twins at Saint Vincent's. Marshall and his sister, Marsha, were the native English speakers. The other two sets of twins were Cuban: Andrés and Santiago, and then Marco and Mateo. The last two had a sister, Sandra. Sandra and Marsha were in D4 with my sister. Sandra was Norma's best friend. As it turned out, Sandra was the last Cuban child to leave the orphanage. She was there until September 1965.

There was Marshall, who was short and stocky, with a lot of energy. He always had a smile on his face. Marshall and Favian were best friends.

Then there was Gabriel, a Cuban boy who spoke fluent English with what appeared to me as perfect pronunciation. When I came to Saint Vincent's, Gabriel had already been there for about eight months. He often translated for the kids who had just arrived. The name Gabriel is the same in English and Spanish, but because native English speakers found Gah-bree-*ehl* difficult to pronounce, Gabriel made the decision to be called Gabe.

This brings to mind an interesting Gabe story.

One day, a bunch of Cubans were hanging out in the playground under a tree, discussing life in the orphanage and the acquisition of this crazy language called English.

"I've learned five hundred words in English!" one of the boys proclaimed.

"Five hundred?" I exclaimed. "How in the world will I ever learn five hundred words in English?"

Londri interjected, "That's only half the battle." After two and a half months in the orphanage, he was beginning to get the hang of English. "Learning words is great, but you have to be able to hold a decent conversation in English."

"Oh yeah?" said one of the boys. "Do you have any idea how long that will take?"

"Three months," claimed Gabe. "You will all be speaking English within three months. That's how long it took me."

"No way!" Another boy shared the skepticism. "I just don't see that happening."

"Mark my word," Gabe assured us. "Look, we have the benefit of living here. We go to school here, and we hear English all the time. All you have to do is communicate."

"I do that," an incredulous listener declared, "and I make all kinds of mistakes."

"Believe me, that's the way to do it," Gabe said confidently. "Learn by making mistakes. Don't be afraid to make them. Go ahead! Speak broken English, mistakes and all. That's how I did it."

"But they laugh at us."

"And you laugh right along with them. Turn it into a game. Make it fun!" Gabe looked at us solemnly. "Three months," he claimed again. "You will all be speaking English within three months."

Gabe was right. Within three months, we were all speaking English well enough to maintain a decent conversation. Within six or seven months, we all spoke English almost as fluently as we spoke Spanish. For some of the kids, English ultimately became the preferred mode of communication.

In many ways, Gabe had become our mentor—something like an inspirational guru. He was always giving us guidance and advice.

"By the way," he once warned us, "it's quite possible that someday you may receive a telephone call from your parents. When that happens, be careful what you say. Don't compromise your mom and dad by speaking against Fidel or socialism. For your parents' safety, assume that the Communists are listening. And let me assure you, they *are* listening."

⊙ ⊙ ⊙

THE OLD NUN AND THE FROG

The science teacher was an old nun; she taught the seventh and eighth graders. One day, she emerged onto the boys' playground, holding a white cloth in her left hand and a frog in a handkerchief with her right while balancing a large glass jar between her left arm and chest. She sat on one of the picnic benches and carefully placed the white cloth down. Positioning the jar next to the white cloth, she summoned us in a gentle voice.

"Come, children, gather round!"

By then, I had been in the orphanage for about two months and comprehended quite a bit of English.

As we circled the bench where she sat, she stated, "Watch now, children. I am going to conduct a scientific experiment. As you may have observed, I brought a jar and I am holding a frog in my hand. The scientific question is, does chloroform act as anesthesia?"

She continued in her docile voice, "You may be asking yourselves, *What is she going to do?*" She showed us a piece of cotton. "This cotton ball is soaked with chloroform." She tossed the cotton ball in the jar and said, "Now watch what happens when I throw the frog in the jar, along with the chloroform-saturated cotton ball."

She threw the frog in the jar.

"The frog is trying to get out of the jar. As you can see, it keeps jumping. Up and down it goes, but to no avail."

The frog was indeed jumping up and down and trying to get out of the jar.

"Alas, it is not able to free itself," she continued, gently. "The poor little feller will soon succumb to the effects of the chloroform."

The frog suddenly lay still. One of the boys said, "It's dead!"

"Oh, no," the nun said quietly, "it is merely asleep. Who remembers the question?"

One of the boys replied, "Will chloroform act like anesthesia?"

"You're a very astute young man." She smiled. "And you have been paying attention." The boys laughed.

Another boy said, "I think that chloroform does act like anesthesia."

"You are very correct," she said. "Allow me to demonstrate."

She put on surgical gloves and showed us a small, thin knife, announcing in her delicate voice, "We are going to cut it open so that we can perceive its organs. But do not be concerned; our little friend won't feel a thing. Remember, that's the answer to our scientific question."

She laid the frog on its back on top of the white cloth, placed the knife below its neck, and sliced it down, opening its belly.

Blood gushed out of the frog, and I thought I was going to get sick. I turned away but couldn't completely. Some of the other boys looked queasy.

"This is the liver, and this is the digestive system." She pointed to those parts of the anatomy.

I had to force myself to look, as did many of the boys. Wyatt's face was white as a ghost. He looked like he was about to faint.

The old nun continued. "The digestive system is responsible for breaking down and absorbing nutrients." I really don't remember her saying that, but it sounds like something she would have said.

She went on, "Let's take a close look at the heart." She took the knife and a pair of pincers, cut the artery of the heart, and took the heart right off with the pincers! She lifted the heart so that we could all see it.

I was getting woozy. A couple of boys turned away, nauseated, but three or four were completely into it—probably future surgeons.

"Poor little creature," she said in her soft and delicate voice. "It has now departed this world. It gave up its life in the name of science."

Then she said, "Now let's take a close look at the brain."

This is the point where I had to walk away. I went to the bushes and nearly puked my entire inners out.

Poor harmless, innocent, little frog! She implied that it gave up its life for the benefit of science. Did it really? Did it willingly give up its spirit? And that little old nun, so soft spoken, so innocent looking. She slaughtered a frog!

◉ ◉ ◉

WYATT, OUR RESIDENT BULLY

One particular episode involving Wyatt stands out in my memory. It occurred in the refectory and changed the way Marshall perceived him.

Wyatt had his customary angry disposition. As we entered the refectory for breakfast, for no reason at all he started pushing some of the little kids around.

Without realizing it, he shoved Marsha, Marshall's twin sister.

She voiced her displeasure loudly. "Stop pushing me, you stupid jerk!"

Calling Wyatt a jerk was bad enough, but he really did not like being called stupid.

"Who you calling stupid?" he demanded of Marsha, and he pushed her again.

Marshall had not seen Wyatt push his sister the first time, but he saw him push her the second time, and he heard her complaining. He ran to her aid. Looking at both Marsha and Wyatt, he asked, "What's going on?"

One of the nuns took notice of the incident, as did some of the kids.

"He pushed me!" Marsha complained.

"Hey, Marshall," Wyatt said, "I didn't notice it was your sister."

"You've been pushing all the little kids around!" Marsha protested.

"I didn't mean to push Marsha. It was an accident."

"Oh yeah?" Marsha persisted. "So it's okay to push the other little ones, right?"

"She's right, Wyatt." Marshall suddenly turned on Wyatt. "Why do you have to keep picking on the little ones, anyway?"

The nun who witnessed what was happening motioned to two other nuns. Many of the other kids also turned to watch.

Wyatt didn't know how to respond to Marshall's criticism. He scratched his head and said, "Gee, Marshall, I don't know. That's what we do, you know? We're the bigger kids. We're in charge. Right?"

"No, that is not what *we* do, Wyatt, that is what *you* do," Marshall countered. "It's not right, especially when you attack my sister."

"I didn't attack her! Besides, I said I'm sorry. All right?"

"No, you did not say you're sorry!" Marshall shouted. "You know what, Wyatt? I am the one who's sorry. I'm sorry that I was ever your friend!"

It seemed as if the whole community was fixated on the unfolding drama. Every child's mouth was wide open.

"Oh yeah?" Wyatt pushed Marshall. "How do you like that? You moron!"

The three nuns quickly approached the two boys.

At that moment, Marshall slapped Wyatt on the cheek and yelled, "How do *you* like that? You double moron!"

Wyatt threw a soft retaliatory punch at Marshall, and Marshall countered with another soft punch. They stared at each other angrily, face-to-face. It seemed as if they did not really want to fight. They swapped a few more punches; soft ones at first, then with a little more force.

Suddenly, it turned into a real fight. All the kids were watching now, in shock.

At this point, the three nuns intervened, separated the boys, and ushered them out of the refectory. Another nun went to Marsha and spoke with her quietly, escorting her out of the refectory.

Wyatt's brother had not seen the whole confrontation from the beginning, but he became keenly aware of the proceedings and started following Wyatt and Marshall. Another nun approached Favian, they exchanged a few words, and she led him from the refectory as well.

Word spread like wildfire among all the children at the orphanage. And the word was that Wyatt and Marshall were interviewed by Mother Superior first, and then she spoke with Marsha and Favian separately.

One of the kids who sat at our table cried out, "¡Huyé!" (ooh-*yeh*)—which is one of many ways to say "wow" in Cuba. "Did you see how Marshall charged full steam ahead?"

Another kid exclaimed, "¡Contrá!"—another way to say "wow." "I'm telling you, he's like a Sherman tank!"

"What's a Sherman tank?" I asked.

"You never heard of a Sherman tank?" Marco looked at me incredulously. "Where've you been?"

Londri came to my rescue. "Sherman tanks were one of the greatest and most powerful American tanks during World War Two."

"Oh, Sherman tanks," I said. "Yeah, I knew that."

"No, you didn't," Marco murmured.

Londri came to my rescue again. "I agree, Marshall sure came out charging like a Sherman tank!"

From then on, many of the kids referred to Marshall as "the Sherman tank."

We never learned about Mother Superior's interview with Wyatt and Marshall or her subsequent conversations with Marsha and Favian. The word, however, was that Wyatt and Marshall shook hands, and then they hugged Marsha and Favian.

Although Marshall and Wyatt remained on friendly terms, their relationship was never the same. Things went back to normal at the orphanage, except Wyatt briefly behaved like an angel—well, a fallen angel. Wyatt being Wyatt, such angelic behavior could not last forever.

This incident changed Marshall's outlook on the new arrivals. He began to see the Cubans in a more positive light; the same could be said of Favian.

◉ ◉ ◉

THE INFIRMARY

I woke up one day not feeling quite right. I went to Mass in the morning and just drank milk at breakfast. Then I went to class, but I was dragging and feeling lethargic. Sister Kevin noticed. She came to my desk and placed her hand on my forehead.

"You have a temperature," she informed me. "You're sick, Antonio."

The next thing I remember was waking up in the infirmary. It was dark. I don't remember how I got there. Another boy was snoring away in the bed next to mine. A nun entered the room with a glass of water and some pills, which I gulped down. She took my temperature.

"You still have a fever, Antonio. Try to go back to sleep."

I must have slept for two whole days, maybe three. A nun would come into the room from time to time to give me some pills and take my temperature and pulse. On the last day there, I noticed that the other boy was gone. I spotted some plastic toy soldiers in a corner of the room, about three inches in height, just like the ones I had in Cuba, except that these were white. I got out of bed and started playing with them.

After a while, a nun entered the room.

"You must be feeling better, Antonio," she said and took my temperature. When she removed the thermometer from my mouth she declared, "Yep, fit as a fiddle!"

"Aw."

"Get dressed, kiddo. You're ready to join the world."

"May I keep one of the soldiers?" I asked, holding the one who stood at attention with his arms at his side, adding, "Just for a little while."

"Well, I don't know."

"Yes," I said, lowering my head. "I understand." And I put the soldier back in its place.

"Listen," she replied, smiling, "you may borrow that one. But you must return it." And she winked at me.

Photos

Norma and Tony with Mom (Nona) and Dad (Ñico)

Tony (held by Tía Elvira) at his second birthday party; His Mom & Dad are seen above Tía, on her right behind her

Norma and Tony with Mom (Nona) and Dad (Ñico) at the Zoo

Florida City Camp for Refugee Cuban Children

Florida City Camp for Cuban Refugee Children

St. Vincent's Orphanage, Vincennes, Indiana—aerial view showing the water tower

St. Vincent's Orphanage, Vincennes, Indiana

St. Vincent's Orphanage, Vincennes, Indiana—front entrance

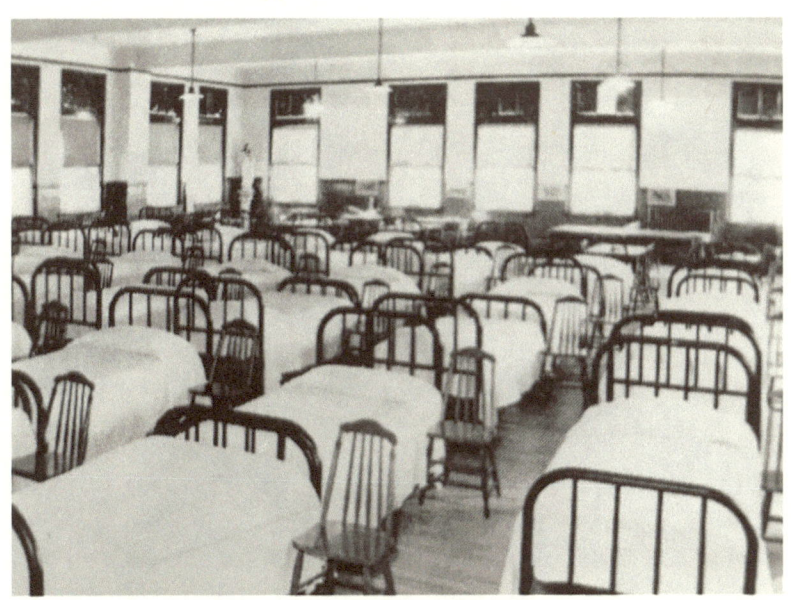

D6 boys' dormitory at St. Vincent's Orphanage, Vincennes, Indiana

Dining Room at St. Vincent's Orphanage, Vincennes, Indiana

D6 boys' lavatory at St. Vincent's Orphanage, Vincennes, Indiana

ST. VINCENT'S ORPHANAGE
The Catholic Boy's Orphanage of St. Vincent's was established in the Highlands two miles out Hart Street Road in 1860 on a 300-acre tract of land. The orphanage housed about a hundred waifs from the diocese of Vincennes, which included most of the state of Indiana. It was operated by the Sisters of Providence and later by the Sisters of St. Francis. The building shown in the picture, built in 1890, was the third structure on the site, two previous ones having been destroyed by fire. The orphanage was torn down in 1975.

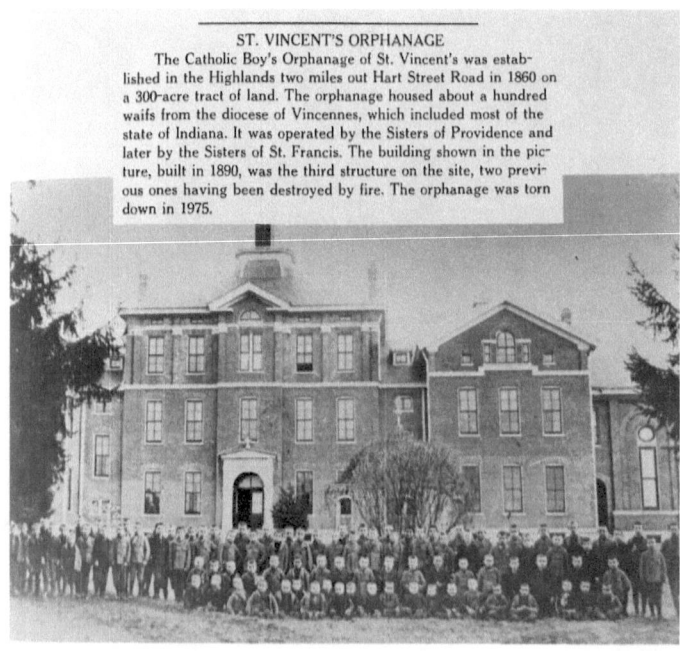

Boys in front of St. Vincent's Orphanage, Vincennes, Indiana

Norma (aged 5) and Tony (aged 7)

Norma and Tony in North Carolina (2022)

PART THREE

Cultivo una Rosa Blanca

Cultivo una rosa blanca
en junio como en enero
para el amigo sincero
que me da su mano franca.
Y para el cruel que me arranca
el corazón con que vivo,
cardo ni ortiga cultivo;
cultivo la rosa blanca.

José Martí

I cultivate a white rose
In June as in January
for the sincere friend
who gives me an honest hand.
And for the cruel person who tears out
the heart with which I live,
I cultivate neither nettles nor thorns:
I cultivate the white rose.

"Cultivo una Rosa Blanca" is a poem written by José Martí about the value of friendship and the importance of cultivating a sincere and pure love with others in order to share ideas, experiences, knowledge, and friendship.

José Martí (1853–1895) was a Cuban poet, essayist, professor, journalist, and publisher. He is known as the apostle of Cuban independence because of his role in the liberation of his country from Spain.

CHAPTER VII

A Saber-Toothed Tiger Tooth!

A few days after my stay in the infirmary, Father So-and-So drove me to the dentist. Three or four other kids went along with us in his car.

Father was not only our priest and our basketball and bowling coach but also our chauffeur. When we were a large group, he was our bus driver. When it was just a few of us, he drove us in his automobile.

I didn't mind going to my general practitioner in Cuba, or to my podiatrist or optometrist, though I sure wasn't crazy about such visits. But I dreaded going to the dentist. I didn't like the idea of someone poking around in my mouth, piercing my teeth with sharp metal instruments.

I decided to take the white toy soldier with me as a type of talisman—for good luck and protection.

I recall waiting in a crowded office. Other than that, I have no memories of my visit to the dentist, except that he kept piercing my teeth with sharp instruments. What I do remember is that when I returned to the orphanage, the kids were on the playground. Favian and Marshall were standing below a large tree about thirty yards away from where Father parked.

Oh, no! I thought. *It's Favian and Marshall, the Sherman tank, for goodness sake!*

As I closed the door behind me and stepped out onto the playground, I wondered whether to make eye contact with them. The Americans and the Cubans were not yet completely comfortable with each other, and although my English was improving, I still felt uneasy about communicating in my new tongue.

How else am I going to learn English, I asked myself, *unless I take a risk?*

Gabe came to mind. *"Go ahead,"* he had encouraged us, *"make mistakes!"*

So I decided to throw caution to the wind. I just had to venture out.

I waved at them, holding the toy soldier in my hand.

They squinted at me and at the toy soldier and they both yelled, "Wow!" at the same time. "Is that your tooth?" Favian yelled.

I thought he wanted to know if I was holding a toy soldier, so I held it up.

"Yeah," I yelled back.

"Holy mackerel!" Marshall exclaimed. "It's a saber-toothed tiger . . . tooth!"

"It's what?" I was mystified.

"Come over here!" Favian shouted, waving me towards them. "Let's take a look at your tooth."

They kept their eyes on the toy soldier as I approached them. Once they perceived that what I was holding was not my tooth, they broke out in laughter.

Favian exclaimed, "We thought that was your tooth!"

"It's so big that we thought it was, like, like, a saber-toothed tiger tooth!" Marshall added.

"Huh?" I showed them the toy warrior. "It's a soldier."

Still laughing, they slapped me heartily on the shoulders.

"What's so funny?" I asked. Then, suddenly, the humor dawned on me, and I joined in on the laughter. Although I was not yet fluent in English, I could now maintain a decent conversation in my new language.

Marshall grabbed the toy soldier from my hand, held it up, and declared ceremonially, "Hear ye! Hear ye! I hereby proclaim that this creature shall henceforth be known, herewith and forthwith, from now on, in perpetuity, as a saber-toothed tiger tooth!"

Wow! I understood most of what he said! Well, sort of; I got the gist. It helped that in class there was a picture book with illustrations of saber-toothed tigers and these creatures were discussed in class. I also remembered hearing and reading the expressions *henceforth, herewith,* and *forthwith* and *in perpetuity* in class, as well as *Hear ye! Hear ye!*

Well, well, well. I was learning English!

Marshall had a flair for the dramatic. He hunched his back, arched his arms over his shoulders, and started barking, trying to imitate a saber-toothed tiger.

"You're barking like a dog, Marshall," Favian said. "Saber-toothed tigers don't bark."

"Well, Favian, what sound do they make?" Marshall asked in a wise-guy sort of way.

"How would I know, Marshall?" Favian retorted in the same tone. "Saber-toothed tigers are extinct!"

"So, who's to say that they didn't bark?"

"You're making a baseless and ridiculous assumption, my dear boy. Saber-toothed tigers are not dogs."

"Well, Favian, my assumption is that they did bark, and you can't prove that they didn't."

"Marshall." Favian shook his head in frustration. "Saber-toothed tigers are cats!"

"Meow."

"Oh brother! They are big cats, Marshall, not little house kittens."

Marshall hunched his back again, arched his arms over his shoulders, and meowed as loud as he could, trying to imitate a big cat.

"Oh yeah," Favian quipped. "Like that's going to unleash the fear of God onto all the animals in the jungle!"

Marshall sighed, looked at me, shrugged, and asked in perfect Spanish, "En español, Antonio, ¿cómo se dice . . . 'saber-toothed tiger'?"

I gave him a puzzled look. "¡Yo qué sé!"

Marshall seemed confused. "What does that mean?"

"It means, 'I have no idea.' Also, it means, 'How should I know?'" I had learned enough English to translate the expression.

Marshall repeated, "¡Yo qué sé!"

"¡Qué sé yo!" I added that one. "You can say it that way too."

"Wait a minute," wondered Favian, "then what does '*Yo no sé*' mean?

Marshall jumped in. "That's easy, Favian, my boy! 'Yo no sé' means 'I don't know'!"

Favian put his index finger to his lip. "Shut up, Marshall!" He turned to me and asked, "Antonio, ¿cómo se dice 'tiger' en español?"

"*Tigre*." I repeated it slowly. "*Tee*-greh."

They both said, "Tigre."

Marshall asked, "¿Y cómo se dice 'sabre-toothed'?"

I pointed to my teeth. "These are *dientes,* but how you say saber-tooth? *¡Qué sé yo!*"

Then I noticed a line of ants walking up and down the tree trunk and pointed to them. "*Hormigas.* How do you say *hormigas* in English?"

"Ants."

"Ants?" I scratched my head. "Like aunts and uncles?"

"Yeah," Marshall laughed, "exactly like aunts and uncles, but totally different!"

Favian slapped Marshall on his shoulder, laughing. "Exactly like aunts and uncles but totally different! That's a good one! You're a genius, Marshall!"

Marshall looked solemnly at Favian. "I heard it on television."

"How do you spell"—I pointed to the line of ants walking up and down the tree—"*ant*?"

Favian replied, "A-n-t."

"And how do you spell *aunt*?" I wondered. "Like, we have an *aunt* and an uncle."

Marshall chimed in. "The same way: a-n-t."

Favian smacked Marshall on his back. "No, Marshall, that's not how you spell it!"

"Well, Favian, pray tell, how do you spell *aunt* like in *aunt* and uncle?"

"A-u-n-t," replied Favian. "Any moron knows that!"

"You're wrong, Favian!"

"No, I'm not! *You* are wrong!"

"You know what? Who cares?" I said and pointed to the basketball court. "Let's shoot some baskets."

"That's the best idea you've had in the longest time, Antonio," Favian complimented me. "Congratulations, kiddo!"

And off we went to the basketball court, with the back-and-forth between Favian and Marshall continuing.

"You're still wrong, Favian!"

"No, I'm not! *You* are wrong!"

"I am not! You are!"

"You are both acting like kids," I blurted out in exasperation.

"That's because, my dear Antonio," Marshall responded, "we *are* kids!"

The three of us burst out laughing so hard that tears streamed from our eyes. In my case, my tears were of immense joy—an awareness that I was acquiring proficiency in English, and an affirmation that I had just sealed a friendship with two great kids.

As for the toy solider . . . *¡Qué sé yo!*

◎ ◎ ◎

THE WINE CAPER

As I have mentioned before, every day commenced in the chapel with the Eucharist—that is, the Mass. Quite a number of the boys were altar boys, as I was. One day, Father and Mother Superior summoned us.

The head nun spoke first. "The sacramental wine that we use for consecration during Mass has been somewhat . . . depleted." She scanned the boys standing in front of her with stone-cold eyes.

"We suspect that some of you boys may know something about this," the priest said. "Am I right?"

I couldn't imagine why anyone would want to do such a thing! I had never been tempted to take illicit sips of wine. The fact is that I really was a good boy. I always did what I was told—well, almost always—and I never gave my superiors an attitude—well, almost never.

"Is it possible," Father speculated, "that some of you boys may have helped yourselves to the sacramental wine?"

Father and Mother Superior crossed their arms and fixed their eyes on each of us as we stood in nervous silence. Their gaze scanned slowly back and forth, in slow motion, trying to pry a confession from the guilty. But try as they might, neither Father nor Mother Superior could get any of the boys to divulge the names of the culprits.

Wyatt, who also was an altar boy, suddenly yelled, "Cubans!"

Well, that was par for the course with Wyatt.

Then his eyes rested accusingly on me.

I faced the priest and defended myself. "Not me, Father!" I turned to Mother Superior and reiterated my innocence. "It wasn't me, Mother."

Shaking her head, Mother Superior glared at Wyatt and quietly said, "Wyatt." Then she turned to the priest and suggested, "Perhaps we should take this up with the larger community. Maybe they can give us a clue about who—"

"That may not be necessary, Mother," the priest interrupted her and turned his attention to us. "Boys, should one of you be guilty, search your soul and come to me. Confess your sin and do penance. Like the good Lord, I too will be merciful. Whatever you confess to me shall remain in the private domain, in the strictest confidence, under the seal of the Holy Sacrament of Confession. I just want you to know that my door is always open to any and all of you."

Boy, he really knew how to lay it on thick!

And it worked.

Word got around the whole orphanage that the guilty parties did confess to Father. Furthermore, Father dispensed penance in the form of having to recite, right then and there in the chapel, kneeling before the altar, the five Sorrowful Mysteries of the Holy Rosary. That could take at least thirty minutes!

As it turned out, Wyatt was one of the guilty. The only reason his name was made public was because he himself revealed it—not because he was sorry for drinking sacramental wine but because he bragged about it to everyone at his table.

● ● ●

When we Cubans first made an appearance in the orphanage, the nuns sat us together in the refectory. Once we started to learn English, however, the tables were arranged in a more inclusive way. By now I had been at Saint Vincent's for almost three months. Kieran and Peter, two Canadian boys, now sat at our table, intermingled among Cuban and American kids.

"This is proof that you can't keep secrets here at Saint Vincent's," Kieran announced to our table when we were having dinner. He was referring to the wine caper.

"If you wanna keep a secret," Peter joined in, "don't tell nobody."

Kieran turned to Peter and corrected him. "Don't tell *any*body."

"Thank you so much for correcting my erroneous error," replied Peter, "Professor English Grammar Professional."

"By the same token, you can't say 'erroneous error,' my fellow Canadian," Kieran corrected him once more. "That's redundant."

"Redun-what?"

"Redundant. That means that it's superfluous, unnecessary."

"Where'd you learn such big words, anyways?"

"In class, you moron! Don't you ever pay attention?"

"Also, it is incorrect to say 'wanna,'" Londri added. "The correct form is 'want to.'"

"You can also say, 'Tell *no* one,'" I ventured to add. "You have to watch your double negatives!"

Marshall happened to be walking by our table when Londri and I were explaining the correct usage of the English language. He congratulated us. "Way to go, guys!" Then he added, jokingly, "Sister learning you real good, ain't she?"

Kieran yelled at Marshall as he left, "The correct form, Marshall, my dear fellow, is to say, 'Sister *is teaching* her students quite well.'"

Marshall just laughed and kept walking away.

Londri leaned forward to whisper in English, "Look at that, the Sherman tank just paid us a compliment!"

Kieran looked at us in amazement. "Well, well, well, you two sure are learning your new lingo."

Londri smiled and said in jest, "*Seester* learnin' us real good."

Grinning, I replied, "Jess!"

The guys at the table broke out in laughter, and Kieran slapped Londri and me on the shoulders.

⊚ ⊚ ⊚

LITURGIES

Our daily ritual included not only attending Mass every morning in the chapel but also reciting Evening Prayer before supper, also in the chapel. On the cusp of Vatican Two, Mass was still celebrated in Latin, not in the vernacular.

The Second Vatican Council was in session from October 11, 1962, through December 8, 1965. It replaced Latin with the vernacular in an attempt to make the Eucharist—which we always called Mass—more comprehensible to the faithful. That way, everyone would hear their own native tongue and understand the words' significance.

I can't say that I remember much about liturgies in the chapel, but I do remember the phrase *Orate Fratres*, which means "Pray, Brethren" or "Pray, Brothers and Sisters." The priest would start off with that phrase, then go on saying, in Latin, ". . . that my sacrifice and yours may be acceptable to God, the almighty Father."

One of the Cuban altar boys jokingly changed the end of the congregation's response to "Huevos fritos con tomates"—meaning "Fried eggs with tomatoes." Hilarious, and it also rhymed. Of course, we never really said this during Mass. We would not dare be that disrespectful—at least, most of us. However, it did make breakfast, the meal that came after Mass, a funny occasion.

Another note on this pre–Vatican Two era is that we had altar *boys*, not altar *girls*. Females were not yet allowed to serve on the altar. The introduction of altar girls came after the Second Vatican Council.

◉ ◉ ◉

THE ALTAR BELL

As in many churches, the altar boys at Saint Vincent's wore black cassocks with white surplices, and we vested in the sacristy. With the influx of Cubans, we had plenty of altar boys. Four of us typically took turns serving at the altar during the Eucharist, all with different tasks. We also took turns at ringing the bell, first during the consecration of the Body of Christ, then during the consecration of the Blood of Christ.

We called it the altar bell, but it actually was a small, handheld set of four bells which produced a delightful sound. There are many types of altar bells. Ours was rung by swiveling it gently and continuously in a left and right motion as the priest held up the host at the consecration, which was transformed into the Body of Christ. After this, the priest would hold up the chalice, and the wine it contained was transformed into the Blood of Christ.

This is what we, as Roman Catholics, believed.

The consecration is not purely Roman Catholic, though. Many Protestant denominations celebrate the consecration in their liturgies, though the precise way in which it is enacted may differ, as well as the particular theological viewpoints, depending on the specific denomination.

I looked forward to the day when I would be the one to ring the bell. The day finally arrived—or so I thought. I took the bell and swiveled it left and right ever so softly. Favian was kneeling next to me. He glanced at me and smiled.

"That was beautiful, Antonio," he said.

Londri was one of the altar boys that day. When we were getting ready to assist with Communion, he came close to me and whispered, "What did you do to make the bell sound so nice?"

I gave him a surprised look. "What do you mean?"

"The bell made a lovely sound, Antonio."

"Really?"

"Yes, it was beautiful! What did you do?"

"I don't know, Londri." I shrugged.

"Well, you did something special!"

"I was an altar boy in Cuba, and in Florida City, too. I guess I have—what would you call it—experience?"

Londri elbowed me on the ribs. "Yeah," he chuckled, "that's exactly what you have: experience."

Right after Mass, some of the kids went to the sacristy to commend me on having rung the bell so beautifully. It felt good to be complimented, but I didn't know exactly what I had done to produce such a marvelous sound, and I was never able to replicate it. The reason was quite simple. I became so self-conscious about it that any attempt was doomed to failure.

It was one of those mysteries of life.

Well, let's get back to that day. After Mass, we went to the refectory for breakfast. Norma approached me and said, "You have become very popular, Tony! Everybody loved the way you rang the bell."

"So I've heard, Norma, but I'm not sure what I did that was so special."

"Well, one of the girls is crazy about you."

"Huh?"

Then I noticed Melody, a very pretty girl about two years younger than me. She was gazing at me with adoration. When our eyes met, her face turned red, and she smiled bashfully. I spun away, my own face warm. Norma looked at me, nodded, and smiled.

Londri, Favian, and Marshall noticed. They were not smiling. I guess every generation is different, but at Saint Vincent's Orphanage, we boys had this unwritten and unspoken rule that we were not supposed to like girls. Regardless, the hormones were kicking in.

What is going on? I pondered. *I'm way too young to be thinking about girls! That's for grown-ups.* She sure was pretty, though. In fact, Melody's name was music to my ears.

At any rate, I suddenly became popular with the other kids. Except for one particular person. As always, Wyatt was the proverbial thorn in the side. He approached me after Mass as I was about to sit at my table, his face red with anger.

"It was my brother's turn to ring the bell, stupid! You cheated him!" And he pushed me on the way to his table.

Favian saw the assault and yelled, "Stop being so mean, Wyatt!"

I went to his table. "I'm sorry, Favian, I didn't know it was your turn."

"I'm glad you rang the bell. You did a great job."

Marshall complimented me, "Real nice, Antonio!"

Marco and Mateo were watching. Marco smiled and said in a low tone, "Looks like the Sherman tank also enjoyed your jingle."

Noticing Marco and Mateo eyeing him, Wyatt stomped over to our table and hollered, "Who you looking at?" And he pushed them.

On the way back to his table he brushed against Andrés and Santiago and stopped to glare at them eyeball to eyeball, trying to intimidate them. Then he pushed them as well.

"Stop being so mean, Wyatt!" Favian hollered at his brother once more.

"It was your turn!" Wyatt shouted at Favian.

"I didn't mind. Besides," Favian added, "Antonio did such a beautiful job!"

"Yeah, beautiful." Wyatt dismissed Favian with a wave of his hand as he arrived at his own table. "Sure."

"Wyatt!" One of the nuns had witnessed Wyatt's behavior, and she gave him a stern look. Wyatt just shrugged.

After a brief moment of silence, the nuns raised their hands to just below their shoulders, and we all stood at our tables to bless the meal. As always, we made the sign of the cross, then recited the prayer to bless our meal. We made the sign of the cross again and took our seats.

Typically, breakfast consisted of oatmeal. Some of the kids poured salt on it. I did not like oatmeal at first, but I eventually warmed up to it. Sugar, butter, and a little milk made it much more palatable than plain old salt.

We also had toast with a stick of butter on the side at every table. A few kids applied such a thick layer of butter that it hid the toast from view and looked like they were eating plain butter! One of the kids used to say lightheartedly, "I like a little toast with my butter."

We must have had eggs and bacon or fruit from time to time, but I can't remember having any of it—not even cold cereal. Bacon and eggs would have been rather expensive. We were too young for coffee or tea. We drank milk. We may have had orange juice, but I don't recall having any.

After breakfast we proceeded to our regular schedule of chores, class, playground, and meals, followed by R&R in the rec room, then to the TV room for some wholesome entertainment. We had a black-and-white television set with only four or five channels and no remote control and no cable. Cable TV had not yet been invented. Color television sets and remote controls existed, but they were super expensive.

We retired for the night between nine and ten o'clock. That was quite a schedule. The nuns ran a tight ship!

☉ ☉ ☉

SISTER KEVIN

Not only was Sister Kevin in charge of the D6 boys, but she was also our teacher. She taught three grades in the same classroom at the same time—grades four, five, and six—to both genders. I was in fifth grade. My guess is that there were about sixty kids in the room, if not more. She divided the class into three groups and took turns teaching each grade while the other two grades were busy working on a task. Sometimes she taught the same lesson to all three grades, depending on the subject matter. She also had the overwhelming task of teaching non-English speakers.

Sister Kevin taught us all the same way, whether we were Cubans or native speakers of English. And we just . . . learned! We learned by listening and repeating. The Cubans acquired proficiency through osmosis—or so it seemed.

We sometimes gathered on the playground to marvel at how we sometimes understood what was being said even though the vocabulary being used was completely new to us.

"How is that possible?" one of the kids once asked.

Well, let's give the awesome power of the human brain its due. As I have mentioned before, all of us learned English within three months, at least well enough to hold a satisfactory conversation. The longer we lived in the orphanage, the more fluency we acquired. The challenge was to attain a truly American English accent. Still, I would say that within six months, we all spoke English nearly as well as the native speakers. After all, children our age—no matter what the country or language may be—are still developing the sophistication and erudition of their own native tongue necessary to function as an adult.

"Just think about it," one of the Cuban kids said. "How did we learn our own language? For that matter, how do babies learn their native tongue?"

Another boy answered, "Well, they listen and they listen, and then they listen and listen some more."

"That's right," another one rejoined. "Then they try to imitate the sounds of spoken language."

"And before you know it," added someone else, "children understand what is being said, and they begin to speak."

"How is this possible?" I asked.

"It's possible because of the amazing power of the brain," Gabe remarked. "It's a mystery, really."

It's . . . *magic.*

Keep in mind that at the orphanage we had the advantage of listening to English all the time. We learned English in the classroom and we learned English by watching movies and television programs, and just by interacting with people. We learned by conversing with our classmates, the nuns, and other staff. If we wanted to speak, we had to convey our thoughts through the use of English.

We also had the advantage, every now and then, of repetition—that is, hearing a lesson that we had already learned in Cuba, but now in English.

Notwithstanding, there was a secret element to our success.

Sister Kevin was a magician.

◉ ◉ ◉

THE FIGHT BY THE SWINGS

We had a terrific playground. It offered us so many opportunities to have fun that we could easily avoid interfering with anyone. We had a basketball court and a baseball field, lots of room in which to play war games or just run around. We had slides, seesaws, merry-go-rounds, and monkey bars. And we had swings—four or five sets of them. There were picnic tables where we could just sit and talk or play cards and board games. But kids didn't want to sit around. That's what old people did. We wanted the freedom to dash, dart, and race wherever and whenever.

I was particularly fond of the swings. One of us would sit on a swing chair while our companion pulled us back as far as the swing would go and push us forward, or just let go and allow gravity to do its job. I loved doing it myself—pulling back as far as possible and letting go. That would propel me forward, then back. The motion would be repeated, going as high as I could, back and forth.

Londri and I often dared each other to see who could go higher. We would do this all day, and once we got tired of the swings, we would do something else.

One day, the twins Marco and Mateo came over to the swings and challenged Londri and me. "Hey," said Marco, "bet we can go higher than you can."

"Oh yeah?" Londri replied.

"Yeah!" Mateo snapped back.

"There is no way you can beat us," I said. "We are the champs at this."

Marco rejoined, "Wanna bet?"

"Sure!" Londri accepted the challenge. "Let's see what you can do."

Just like that, the four of us were swinging up and down, laughing hysterically and having a good time.

All of a sudden, Mateo stopped unexpectedly, got off his swing, stood up, and stared at me. He pulled his swing sideways and let it go just as I was rolling by. It smacked me right on the head so fiercely that it knocked me off the swing. I lost consciousness for an instant. After a few seconds, I knelt and held my head. It hurt like crazy! I wiggled my head to shake off the cobwebs. I tried to get up but couldn't. I was in shock.

My glasses had also been knocked to the ground. Londri picked them up and handed them to me. He yelled at Mateo, "What's wrong with you? Why did you do that for?"

Mateo shrugged. "I," he stammered, "I don't know." He seemed to be in shock, too. I could see that he hadn't meant it.

The incident attracted a crowd of kids, and they came running over. One of the boys demanded, "You gonna let 'im get away with that?"

Another one shouted, "Ya gotta get even, Antonio!"

Mateo just stood there, mouth wide open in amazement.

Londri helped me up. I stood slowly, still woozy and holding my head.

A third kid yelled, "Ya gotta fight!"

I shook my head. "I'm not a fighter."

"What are ya . . . chicken?"

One of the unspoken rules in the esoteric, secret realm of kid-dom is that you never ever want to be classified as being chicken.

"No," I retorted. "I'm not chicken!"

Another one said, "Well then, fight!"

More kids surrounded us. Someone yelled, "Fight!" Others echoed the sentiment.

One of the kids pushed Mateo forward. Another did the same to me. Mateo and I stood in the middle of a circle, facing each other. Suddenly, all the kids were yelling, "Fight, fight, fight!"

Mateo held his dukes up like a boxer. Someone pushed me again and dared me, "Come on, let 'im have it!"

I took off my glasses, gave them to Londri, and held my dukes up as well. Mateo and I stared at each other. The chant became unrelenting: "Fight, fight, fight!"

The peer pressure was too powerful. I threw the first punch, hitting Mateo squarely on the nose. He shook his face and stared at me questioningly, holding his nose. He was surprised by my aggression. I threw another punch at his face, then another.

So, he retaliated.

Suddenly, it was warfare!

We circled each other, looking for an opportunity to launch a blow, then unleashed a whole bunch of wild rocket wallops at each other, impulsively, violently.

All boxers get hit, of course, but they are trained to protect their faces as much as possible. Neither Mateo nor I knew how to box nor how to protect ourselves from blows to the face. We were hitting each other and we were getting hit.

The "Fight, fight, fight!" chant was never ending. I had been in a fight before—as most kids have, I suppose—but this was by far the fiercest one up to this point. An animal instinct took over us, and we lost control. Mateo and I had been ferociously going at each other for a few minutes when the chant suddenly came to an end.

Sister Kevin had made an entrance.

She dangled a pair of boxing gloves before us by the strings. Her face revealed her disgust for the gloves, as if they were something repulsive, like two dead rats.

"We only have one set," she declared, "so you have to decide who's going to use the left one and who's going to use the right one." She looked me in the eyes. "Antonio, which one do you want?"

I shrugged in bewilderment, stunned that she was endorsing our belligerence instead of trying to stop it.

Since I didn't answer, she said, "Okay then, you take this one." And she gave me the left glove. I should have opted for the other one since I am right-handed.

We each put on our respective glove.

"Just don't kill each other," Sister Kevin counseled. "It makes things . . . *messy*."

Then she made an about-face and left the scene.

What? That's it? I thought. *No punishment? She just goes away and forgets about it?*

I suspect she realized that neither Mateo nor I were troublemakers. Basically, we were good kids. But the thought lingered in my mind and wouldn't go away. *Wait a minute! Why are we not getting punished?* A frightening premonition came over me. It was quite possible that she would still summon us for a private consultation and mete out a sentence—a painful one.

In the meantime, Mateo and I were still circling each other, albeit reluctantly. We came to a stop and stared at each other in stupefaction. We were both bleeding from the nose. Mateo had a black eye, and my lower lip was swollen, not to mention the bump on my head from getting hit by the swing.

The mob of onlookers had gone stone silent. By now the fight had approached a peculiar phase. I don't know why, but I resumed the struggle and threw a punch. It didn't hit Mateo. He threw one at me. It missed. We jabbed at each other, lackadaisically this time. Occasionally we landed a blow, just to make it look good, but it was a soft one. Mostly, we threw air punches. The spectators could see that the fight was essentially over and started to disperse.

After a moment, I looked at Mateo and said, "This is stupid. Wanna stop?"

"You give up?"

"No, I just want to stop, that's all."

Another one of the unspoken rules of kid-dom is that you never ever surrender. Otherwise you are a yellow-bellied coward.

"I am *not* giving up!" Mateo declared.

"You started it, Mateo! Can't we just say that we're even? Nobody wins and nobody loses. Whatta ya say?"

Mateo considered the proposal for an instant, took off his glove, and threw it on the ground. I took mine off and threw it on the ground as well.

Then we hugged each other.

From then on, Mateo was my best friend. After Londri, that is. Londri would always be my best friend. Ain't nothing like a good fight to cement a strong friendship!

And, as it turned out, neither of us got punished.

How lucky can a kid get?

◎ ◎ ◎

Word got around the entire orphanage that Mateo and Antonio got into a big fight by the swings. We became instant celebrities. A few days later, when Mateo and Marco went to visit their sister, Sandra, Norma was there with her.

Norma addressed Sandra and Marco in a serious tone. "I'm sorry, guys, but Mateo beat my brother up, so now I have to beat him up."

Sandra and Marco looked at each other and nodded in concurrence. They understood these laws.

And so, she did. Norma pushed Mateo against the wall, slapped his face with her right hand, then with her left hand. Norma and Mateo stared at each other momentarily, and then Norma unleashed an attack, slapping him repeatedly with both hands. Mateo held up his arms to protect his face, but he would not strike back.

Another very prominent and critical unspoken rule of kid-dom, one to which all boys must adhere, is that a boy shall never ever hit a girl.

After a few blows, Sandra spoke up. "Okay, Norma, that's enough." And Norma stopped hitting Mateo. Sandra remained Norma's best friend. She realized that Norma had to restore her brother's honor.

"Yep, I clobbered him!" Norma told me when we saw each other in the refectory. "And I'll clobber him again if I have to!"

"But, Norma," I said, "me and Mateo, like, we are good friends now. Gosh, he's my best friend! Well, after Londri."

"I don't care," Norma replied. "I did what I did because I had to do what I had to do."

That's a rather interesting sentence construction, I thought, but decided not to say anything about it.

"Nobody's ever gonna mess with my *big* brother!" She held my face with both hands and avowed, "I promise you, Tony"—she grinned slyly—"*I* will always protect you!"

Norma was coming into her own. She was growing up.

◉ ◉ ◉

DOMINGO

Domingo was one of the last Cubans to arrive at the orphanage. Londri and I immediately hit it off with him.

A few more Cuban children would show up at Saint Vincent's, but Operation Pedro Pan was coming to an end. It finally did a few months later—on October 23, 1962, during the Missile Crisis.

We Cubans tried to make sense of our situation and often talked about it. What exactly happened in our country that landed us in the United States? Although he was a newcomer, Domingo helped us fill in many pieces of the enigmatic puzzle of our exodus—the Cuban diaspora. He was a wealth of information about Fidel Castro and his revolution. He attributed his knowledge to his father.

Londri and I invited Domingo to meet with us under the water tower one day. Gabe joined us, as did the twins Marco and Mateo and Santiago and Andrés, who had decided to be called Andy.

"We know about Fidel's revolution," Londri explained to Domingo. "We know that he kicked Batista out of Cuba and took over the island."

"Yeah," I interjected, "but who, exactly, is this Fidel Castro? Do you know?"

"I know what my father told me," Domingo replied.

We listened to his story and peppered him with questions.

"According to my father," Domingo related, "Fidel Castro is a bastard."

"We know that!" Mateo jumped in.

"I mean that he is illegitimate," Domingo explained. "Deep down—psychologically speaking, that is, according to my dad—Fidel feels that he is inferior to other people. My dad calls it an inferiority complex. Fidel has a need to make himself important. He is the son of a rich man. Fidel's father had five children with his first wife. They got divorced because the old man was cheating on his wife with one of his servants. My father says, if I remember correctly, that she was twenty-seven years younger than Fidel's father."

Santiago interrupted Domingo. "This how you know?"

Santiago had been behaving peculiarly recently. Sometimes he said strange things and acted a little weird. We sort of accepted and went along with it.

He often got his words mixed up. He tried to correct himself now. "I mean, how do you know all this?"

"Well, this is what my father told me."

"Please," Gabe said, "pick up where you left off."

Domingo continued. "Well, Fidel's father and his maid had seven children. I think three were boys. The other four were girls. The first three children were bastards, and Fidel was the third one. That's why *he* is a bastard."

"I knew it!" Santiago exclaimed. "Him bastard for real now we know! I mean, now we know he's a real bastard!"

"Go ahead," Londri prodded Domingo. "Go on with the story."

"Anyway," Domingo picked up the narrative. "They were legally married after Fidel was born. Raúl was their fourth, so he is legitimate."

"Raúl still a bastard is!" Santiago interposed himself once more. He blinked rapidly a few times, shrugged, and shook his head in a quirky motion.

His brother slapped his arm. "Stop interrupting!"

Domingo returned to the tale. "My father told me that it's a big scandal to be born a bastard. That's why Fidel was initially given his mother's last name of Ruz. Eventually his father recognized him. That's when Fidel took the surname of Castro."

"Wow!" Santiago interrupted again. "That I not knew!"

Andy reprimanded him. "You're at it again, Santiago—interrupting!"

"I so sorry am, mister!" Santiago gave his brother a wise-guy answer.

Domingo smiled. "All in all, Fidel's father had thirteen children: five by his first wife and seven by the maid, who became his second wife."

"Five plus seven equals twelve," Marco calculated. "You said thirteen."

"Well, yes. He had another bastard son with a different woman."

"That's why so stupid is he!" Santiago exclaimed.

"Oh, no," Domingo corrected him, "Fidel is a very smart man. He was taught by the Jesuits in Belén."

The Jesuits, officially called the Society of Jesus, is a Catholic religious order of priests and brothers who work as teachers and missionaries. Belén is Spanish for Bethlehem.

"Belén?" Andy scratched his head. "I've heard of Belén, but what is it?"

This time Santiago reprimanded his brother. "Interrupting now are you!"

"¡Cállate, chico!" (Shut up, man!) Santiago sometimes got on Andy's nerves. "I just want to know what Belén is!"

"It's a prominent school," Domingo informed us. "Fidel also studied law and later became a lawyer."

◉ ◉ ◉

SUNDAY

A few days later, Domingo, Londri, and I were on the playground, standing on the landing facing the basketball court. Favian and Marshall approached us with a burning question.

"We just can't figure this out," Favian said.

Marshall blurted out, "Why are so many of you Cubans coming to our orphanage, anyway?"

"Yeah, what's going on in Cuba?"

"We hear it's gone Communist or something," Marshall added. "Is that true?"

Londri and I started to convey to them the story Domingo had related to us when, out of the blue, Marshall turned to Domingo and demanded, "Doesn't your name mean Sunday?"

Domingo looked at me for assistance. He was not yet fluent in English, so I answered for him. "Why, yes," I replied tentatively, "yes, it does."

"That's a funny name for a kid, isn't it?" Favian asked.

"Yes." I scratched my head. "Yes, it is."

Londri translated the conversation for Domingo, who replied in Spanish, "Domingo means Sunday, but it's also the name of a saint. Incidentally, the capital of the Dominican Republic is Santo Domingo."

Londri translated what Domingo told us.

Marshall looked at us quizzically. "Saint Sunday?"

"Is that a real saint?" Favian wanted to know.

Londri and I shrugged.

"Sunday is a day," Londri mulled over the question, "the day after Saturday."

"Really?" I reflected out loud. "I thought it was the day before Monday." Everyone smiled.

"There must be an explanation," Londri said.

I had an idea. "There's a dictionary in the rec room. Why don't we look it up?" I translated the conversation for Domingo.

"I don't believe that a dictionary is going to be of much help," Londri replied. "What we need is an encyclopedia."

"A what?" I didn't know what that was.

"That's right." Favian was thinking out loud. "And there's one of those in the rec room as well."

Londri told Domingo what we were talking about. The five of us bolted into the building and sprinted up the stairs to the second floor. Marshall charged ahead like a bolt of lightning, climbing two and three steps at a time. We reached the second floor and flew into the rec room.

Domingo turned to Londri and me by the doorway and whispered, "No wonder they call him the Sherman tank. Did you see him? It's like he was attacking the flight of stairs!"

"Yeah," I agreed. "With Marshall it's always full steam ahead!"

Londri added, "But he's really nice." The three of us nodded our consensus.

Upon entering the rec room, we noticed a large encyclopedia on the table. We opened it and rapidly flipped through the pages, but we couldn't find the English name for Domingo. I don't think any of us really knew how to look it up. Then we searched in the dictionary and struck out there, too.

"Hey!" Marshall had an idea. "Why don't we ask Gabe? He knows everything!"

"I saw him on the basketball court," I informed the group.

We ran down the stairs again and dashed onto the playground. Gabe was indeed on the basketball court, shooting foul shots by himself.

"Hey, Gabe!" Marshall shouted at him. "We have a question for you."

"Domingo means Sunday, right?" Favian asked.

Marshall queried, "So what is the *name* for Domingo in English?"

"It can't be Sunday," Favian said. "There has to be an explanation."

"You are right; there is an explanation," Gabe responded. "And you are correct, Domingo means Sunday, for the day of the week. However, it is also a name. That name, in English, is Dominick. It comes from the Latin word *Dominus*."

"Latin?" Marshall exclaimed. "Like the language the priest uses at Mass?"

"That's right," Gabe replied. "Sunday really means 'the day of the Lord.' That's why we go to Mass on Sunday—because it's the day of the Lord."

Marshall was amazed. "How do you know that?"

"Because"—Gabe smiled and tapped his temple a couple of times with his index finger—"I'm a smart cookie."

"Wait a minute!" Marshall challenged Gabe. "What are you talking about? We go to Mass every day!"

"The *nuns* go to Mass every day," Favian corrected him. "We just accompany them."

"So," I mused, "the English name of the saint Santo Domingo is . . ."

Londri finished my thought. "Saint Dominick."

Gabe smiled and said, "That's right."

◉ ◉ ◉

THE SHERMAN TANK

A couple of weeks after this incident, Domingo, Londri, and I were again standing on the landing facing the basketball court. As usual, Gabe was shooting baskets on the basketball court by himself. Marshall approached us with another burning question.

"Why are you Cubans calling me the Sherman tank?"

The accusation caught us all by surprise. We didn't know how to respond.

"No, we're not!" I lied.

The other guys shook their heads. Londri said, "We've never called you by that name, Sherman."

"You have so!" Marshall insisted.

"Where did you get that idea?" I asked.

Gabe overheard the conversation and came over. "Come on, fellas," he said, "tell the truth." He apologized. "It's true. We have been calling you the Sherman tank. We're sorry."

"Yeah," Londri agreed. "We're very sorry, and we won't call you by that name again."

"But why?" Marshall asked.

"It goes back to the day Wyatt pushed your sister," Gabe explained, "and the way you went charging to help her."

"Yeah." Domingo struggled with his English. "How you run rapid for Wyatt, you look like Sherman tank."

"Really?" Marshall revealed a slight smirk. "Is that why?"

"Yes, that's why," I responded.

"So, you didn't mean it as an insult to me?"

"No! Never!" Londri said.

"To tell you the truth," I stated, "we meant it as a sign of . . . a sign of . . . What's a good word?"

Gabe finished my sentence. "Respect. As a sign of respect."

"*Oye, viejo*," Domingo declared, "you were good!"

"What'd you say?" Marshall inquired. "Oy what?"

"'Oye, viejo' is a Cuban expression," Gabe explained. "It means, 'Listen, man.' *Oye* means 'hear,' or 'listen.' *Viejo* means 'old man.'"

Londri offered an additional explanation. "What Domingo is saying is that what you did and what you said to Wyatt was really good!"

Marshall scratched his head and looked at us curiously, mouth opened wide.

"What I did was really good?" Slowly, a smile formed on his face, until he was grinning from ear to ear. "All right, I love it!" We all started laughing.

From that day on, Marshall and our little group were enmeshed like brothers.

CHAPTER VIII

Summer

Summer arrived. Regular classes ended, and Sister Kevin went on vacation. Another nun, Sister Cordelia, took charge of the D6 boys. She was a middle-aged woman—older than Sister Kevin—and plain looking. She was nice and took good care of us, but she was not as charismatic as Sister Kevin. In fact, she was nothing like Sister Kevin. Still, there was a certain warmth about her.

Just as Sister Cordelia was now in charge of the D6 boys, another nun made an entrance.

◉ ◉ ◉

SISTER GUADALUPE

Summer school came with the arrival of the sunshine season of 1962 and Sister Guadalupe. She was assigned expressly to teach English to the Cuban children. There must have been around thirty or forty of us at the time. It was hard to tell how many because Cuban kids kept coming and going. Quite a few were sent to live with foster families. We didn't know why some kids were sent to foster homes, and we often wondered if any of us would be sent away. Some lucky kids left because their parents had arrived from Cuba. As always, we learned that they were gone by their absence.

Like Sister Cordelia, Sister Guadalupe was middle aged and plain looking. She spoke fluent English as well as fluent Spanish—with a Mexican accent, which we found quite appealing. We were not familiar with this accent, although we had heard a similar one in movies by Mario

Moreno, who went by the stage name of Cantinflas—a very famous Mexican comic. His films were widely shown in Cuba and throughout Latin America. He played the part of Passepartout in the 1956 film *Around the World in Eighty Days* with David Niven and Shirley MacLaine. He also played the lead role in the 1960 film *Pepe* with Dan Dailey and Shirley Jones.

On the first day of class, Sister Guadalupe introduced herself in Spanish and told us that she was a Mexican American. "Do you know what that is?" We all shrugged. We had no idea.

"Well, I'm here to teach you English," she informed us. "I'll start by telling you a little bit about myself, in English." She pointed to a map of the United States. "You also have to learn about your new country, so let's begin here." She moved her finger to Texas and to the town in which she was born. I can't recall where, but my guess is San Antonio.

I do not recall any of her lessons that summer, either, except that we learned a lot. She not only taught us English but also the history, customs, and traditions of the United States. What I particularly remember is that she played cards and board games with us. She even got on the swings!

And she was exceptionally good at softball—middle aged or not, habit and all.

We didn't have enough baseball gloves to go around, so I played outfield without a glove. That means that I had to catch flyballs barehanded. I eventually learned to open my hands wide, but not soon enough. Why would an outfielder catch a flyball barehanded, with fingers stretched out to boot, instead of catching it on the palm of the hand? That is a reasonable question to ask. I came up with the answer the hard way.

The first time I caught a ball without a glove, my fingers were stretched out. The ball struck my fingertips with the force of an atomic bomb. It hurt like heck! My fingers were swollen and sore for the longest time. I could barely handle utensils when we were eating in the refectory. It made classroom time quite painful and the task of writing virtually impossible. And Sister Guadalupe was sympathetic to my pain.

I wasn't able to play the outfield for a while. I went back out there a week or so later and, like an idiot, I tried catching a fly ball with my fingertips stretched out a second time. This time Sister Guadalupe was even more sympathetic to my pain.

She was the one who hit the flyball.

Once my fingers recovered and I got back in the outfield, Londri reminded me, "Make sure to catch flyballs on the palm of your hands this time, Antonio, or you'll be sorry again!"

And then he laughed! My best friend, laughing at my ineptitude!

Sister Guadalupe told us that she had been playing softball since she was a little girl. Now she played the sport while wearing a habit, which she would simply roll up. She could run around the bases, bat, and field. She really enjoyed the game.

Above all, she loved us. And we loved her.

It was with great sadness that the time came to say goodbye. The summer ended, and Sister Guadalupe had to return to her community. We gave her a wet send-off (wet from our tears) in the baseball field on the pitcher's mound.

It was an extremely emotional, heartfelt farewell.

We had already experienced a few departures. Many more were still to come.

The next one came right away. With the departure of Sister Guadalupe, we learned that Sister Kevin would not be coming back to Saint Vincent's. She was assigned to another school. We wondered whether she'd known about this when she left "on vacation." Perhaps she just couldn't bring herself to tell us.

Sister Kevin wrote us all individual letters, however, telling us how much we were missed. It must have taken her a week or two to write to everyone. If you included the girls who were in her class, in addition to the D6 boys, there must have been between seventy to eighty kids!

Sister Cordelia remained at the helm of the D6 boys. By now we had become familiar with her and accustomed to her ways. We liked her, but Sister Kevin she was not.

What made Sister Kevin so special? She was firm and strict and suffered no fools, and you certainly did not want to cross her or get on her wrong side. Still, there was an endearing warmth about her.

What really mattered was that she cared for us. She truly cared.

◎ ◎ ◎

GARBECH

Sometimes we learned English by trial and error, and in a comical way.

On one particular occasion, we were served a new dish in the refectory. It was delectable! I believe that it was either lasagna or baked ziti. I'm going to say it was lasagna.

"What do you call this dish?" I asked the kids at the table, pointing at it with my fork and my mouth full. "It's so delicious that I would like to have seconds."

Santiago, who was a smart aleck, replied, "It's called garbage."

Wow! I thought. *Santiago actually got the order of his words correctly!* Then I asked, "Gorbech? Could you please say that word one more time?"

"Garbage," repeated Santiago.

"Garbech?"

"That's right."

I raised my hand and waited for one of the nuns to come to our table. I sensed something was amiss because little smirks appeared around me, but I decided to go along. After all, what was the worst that could happen, right?

One of the nuns, Sister Matilda, approached our table. She was quite a character herself—as you may glean by the following scene.

I made my request. "Can I have some more garbech, Sister?"

"I beg your pardon."

"Garbech." I pointed to the remains of the dish on my plate.

"Oh," she said without batting an eye. "You mean *lasagna*, right?"

"Jess." I'd been had!

"Yes, you may have some more. It's called lasagna, Antonio. They . . ." She couldn't hide a very slight grin as she looked at the others. "They are pulling your leg. Garbage means '*basura*.'"

Santiago blinked rapidly and twisted his head left and right in a quick, jerky fashion. Sister Matilda seemed to take note of his demeanor, but she did not address it. Instead, she directed her attention to me.

"By the way, you are pronouncing the word incorrectly. It's like this: *gar*-bage. Say it."

"Gar-bech."

"Look at my lips and say it slowly: *gar*-bage. Try it."

I observed her lips and tried to imitate the pronunciation. "Garbage."

"That's right!" *Wow! I pronounced it correctly*! She pointed to the lasagna. "This is called lasagna. Say it."

"Lasagna. That's not hard," I said.

"Okay, from the top, ask me again."

"Can I have more lasagna?"

"May I."

"Excuse me?" I wasn't sure what she meant.

"May I." She noticed my hesitation. "Try to be polite."

"Oh!" I understood now. "Jess. *May* I have more lasagna?"

"Good. Now try saying it with the magic word."

"The magic word?" I wasn't sure what the magic word was, but I took a shot at it. "You mean . . . please?"

"That's right. Now try it again, from the top."

"May I have some more lasagna, please?"

"You may also use the expression 'a second helping.' Try again."

"May I have a second helping of lasagna, please?"

"Good. What's my name?"

"Uh, Sister Matilda?"

"That's right. One more time now, from the top, with my name this time. Come on!"

Boy, she is having a good time with this.

"May I have a second helping of lasagna, please, Sister?"

She put on a frown. "Sister? Sister *who*?"

"Sister Matilda?"

"You got it! Again, one more time, from the top, with my name."

"May I have a second helping of lasagna, please, Sister Matilda?"

Sister Matilda revealed another slight grin. "Yes, you certainly may, sir! I'll be right back with your order." She turned and went into the kitchen. We could hear her laughing with the other nuns there.

"I think she's having fun!" said one of the boys at the table.

"Not only that, but she said 'basura'!" I exclaimed. "My goodness, the nuns are learning Spanish!" I eyeballed Santiago suspiciously, then scrutinized all of them. "Garbage, really! Sister Matilda is right. You are all pulling my leg!"

Santiago and the kids at the table burst out laughing.

Sister Matilda returned with my second helping of lasagna. "Here's your basura, Mr. Dora. I do hope that you find this second helping acceptable, sir." Another smile crossed her lips.

"Jess."

"Jess? The correct pronunciation is *eeeh-ehsss*. Yes!"

"*Eeeh*-ehsss. Yes, it is, Sister Matilda!" I couldn't help but smile myself. "It is acceptable. Thank you very much!"

"Please, taste it."

I cut a small piece with my knife and took a bite. "Mmm! This second helping tastes even better than the first one!"

"Excellent!" Sister Matilda said, beaming from ear to ear. She retreated into the kitchen. A few seconds later, just as before, we heard laughter.

"Wow, fellas," I exclaimed, with a mouthful of lasagna, "this second helping is way more delicious than the first helping. I'm not kidding."

Gabe looked at me proudly. "What did I tell you when you first arrived here? You'll be speaking English within three months. And you've been here three months!"

"That's right, three months," I agreed.

"Look at that! You're already there, Antonio!" He turned to the other kids sitting at the table and said to them, "Sister Matilda just taught Antonio a superb lesson in the English language. In fact, all of you are, right now, speaking English rather well!" Gabe was beaming. "Didn't I tell you so?"

Gabe was right. What's more, within eight to ten months, English had become the dominant language for many of us, and we spoke it fluently, albeit with a slight accent. Sadly, a small number of the Cuban children forgot Spanish altogether, which made the eventual reunion with their parents fairly difficult.

I myself forgot quite a bit and had to make a concerted effort to recapture my language over the following years; when I was in high school, I took a new course being offered there, Spanish for Native Speakers. It was taught by a foreign language teacher by the name of Mr. Minnelli—no relation to Liza. Mr. Minnelli was an excellent teacher and spoke eight languages. I was very impressed with his linguistic skills. He taught Spanish, French, Portuguese, German, and Russian at our school, alternating the languages from year to year.

Spanish for Native Speakers was so helpful that I was able to regain my Spanish fluency. Today I am equally adept at both English and Spanish.

◉ ◉ ◉

A GREEN BOOGER!

Marshall could not help being Marshall. He was a comedian and had a reputation for breaking out into wacky shenanigans out of the blue.

One day, Marshall was playing basketball with Londri, Favian, some of the other guys, and me. Marshall started double dribbling on purpose.

"Double dribble! Double dribble!" we shouted.

"So?" he yelled back and kept double dribbling.

Favian grabbed the ball out of Marshall's hands. "You want the ball?" He threw it right back at Marshall. "Here! Stop acting like a wise guy and shoot that stupid ball in the basket!"

Marshall took the basketball and stuffed it inside his green T-shirt. "What ball?"

"The ball you're hiding in your T-shirt, you dimwit!"

Marshall started flailing his arms, screaming, "I have a lump in my belly!"

A crowd of kids came over to the landing to watch.

"I ate a watermelon!" Marshall embraced his belly. "A whole watermelon!"

The kids were smiling and pointing at him.

"No! No, that's not true. I did not eat it. I did not chew it." Marshall realized that he had an audience and hammed it up. "I swallowed it!"

The kids were giggling. Favian shook his head. "Oh brother!"

"Wait a minute!" Marshall hugged the ball inside his green T-shirt. "It's . . . it's . . . it's a booger! It's a great, big, green booger!"

The kids were enjoying the show. Favian pleaded with them, "Don't humor him, please!"

Marshall exclaimed, "Oh no! I'm *pregnant*!" The spectators started laughing.

Marshall took off his T-shirt, careful to keep the basketball rolled up inside. Then he unfurled his T-shirt, releasing the ball. The ball hit the ground and bounced several times. Marshall ran after it, cuddled it in his arms, and announced, "Yes, it's a booger, all right! It's a great, big, green . . . booger!" The onlookers cackled hysterically.

Favian smiled and shook his head. He looked at Londri, then at me and the other guys. As if on cue, we all started cracking up, rolling on the ground with merriment.

◉ ◉ ◉

PIE IN THE FACE

As I have expressed previously, I loved Saint Vincent's Orphanage, but not everyone shared my views, especially Santiago, Andy's twin.

For whatever reason, he was unable to adjust to his new surroundings. He seemed to find life away from his family and country quite challenging. For some time now, he had displayed a type of behavior which could only be classified as odd. Sometimes his actions were downright bizarre—like the pie-in-the-face affair.

We had finished supper, and dessert had just been served. Today we were having a special treat: lemon cream pie! We all ogled that delicious-looking pie, licking our lips in anticipation.

Suddenly, Santiago stood and reached for the lemon cream pie. He held it in his hands for a moment, looking at it with confusion. He said in a low voice, "What with this going I am to do?" As he would often do, he blinked rapidly a few times and jerked his head left and right.

Then he announced in a threatening whisper, "Yep, somebody is gonna get this face in the pie." He corrected himself. "I mean, somebody is going to get the pie in the face . . . this pie, in his face."

He scanned the astonished expressions of the kids at the table while balancing the pie in his hands. We all knew that he was crazy enough to pull such a stunt. He looked at me and said, "Will you the one be, Antonio?" I opened my eyes wide with fear. He glanced at Londri and said, "Will you it be?" He turned to Andy. "Maybe at you it I will throw, brother of mine." He took turns looking at everyone, menacing each one with the threat: "You are gonna it maybe get!"

He stared at the pie in his hands for what seemed like an eternity, as if wondering what he was really going to do with it.

All of a sudden, he smashed it right in his face with such force that the contents of the pie scattered all over his nose, his eyes and mouth, his ears, hair, shirt, and the wall behind him. He was completely covered with whipped cream, lemon custard, and graham cracker crust!

Santiago started laughing hysterically, loudly. We all stared at each other, dumbfounded, speechless. Indeed, everyone in the dining room was equally speechless.

Two nuns came over and dragged Santiago away backwards by his arms, his feet trailing along the floor. He kept laughing wildly, frantically, uncontrollably. Andy, who was sitting at the table, lowered his face and covered it with his hands, trying to hide his tears.

Word got around that Santiago was taken to a special school. Within a few days, Andy also disappeared. We were told that he went to live with foster parents.

◉ ◉ ◉

TE QUIERO MUCHO

As I have indicated earlier, Father was our priest. He is the one who said Mass in the morning, heard our confessions, and often led us in evening prayer before supper.

In the summer, he would take us to this huge pool—I mean humongous! It had a depth of about ten feet at its deepest point, with numerous slides and diving boards. In the center was a huge platform with many chairs. People would climb onto the platform and congregate there, staying all day if they wanted to. They could talk, read, sleep—or try to make up their minds about whether to dive into the water.

On one occasion, Londri and I were standing in the pool. A teenage couple heard us speaking a language they did not understand. They swam over to us, and the young man asked, "Excuse me, is that Russian you are speaking?"

"No, honey," said the young girl, "it's German."

"No," said Londri, "it's Spanish."

"Spanish?" The young gentleman seemed confused.

His girlfriend asked, "Where are you from?"

"We're from Cuba," Londri responded.

"Cuba?" The young man looked baffled now.

"But you got blond hair," his girlfriend stated.

"With blue eyes!" he added.

The young lady got close to me to look at my eyes. "No, honey, he's got green eyes."

"Yes, I know," I said, scratching my head. *What are they up to?* I wondered.

"No, not that one, the other one!" He meant Londri. "The other one has blue eyes."

His girlfriend went to Londri and observed his eyes. "That's right, honey. This one has blue eyes."

The young man changed the topic. He looked at us and inquired, "How do you say 'I love you' in your language?"

"Te quiero," Londri answered.

The young man turned to his girlfriend and expressed his love for her: "Te quiero."

"How do you say," she queried, "'I love you very much'?"

"Te quiero mucho," I replied.

They both looked at each other and said, "Te quiero mucho." She giggled.

"How about 'I love you really, really, really very much'?" he probed further.

Londri and I looked at each other inquisitively. Londri informed them, "Yo te quiero muchísimo a ti." He scratched his temple with his index finger. "I guess."

"Yo te quiero moo . . . moo-what?" *Muchísimo* seemed too big a word for the young man.

"What's that word?" the woman asked. "Moo . . . ?"

"What does it mean?"

I tried my best to explain. "Muchísimo means a lot—very much."

"But all you have to say is 'Yo te quiero a ti,'" Londri assured them. "I think that's good enough."

They seemed pleased to hear that. They turned to each other and expressed their love—"Yo te quiero . . . a ti!"—and kissed each other on the lips.

Immediately after conveying his love for her, the young man spun around to face us.

"Cuba, eh? Fidel Castro."

"He's such a nice man!" she exclaimed.

"Oh, no," Londri countered. "He's a bad man."

They both started laughing. "Just kidding!" the young man assured us.

They looked at each other again and said simultaneously, "Yo te quiero a ti." They kissed each other on the lips one more time, made an about-face, and swam away, repeating, "Yo te quiero a ti" to each other over and over again—all the way until they turned a corner beyond the center platform, out of sight.

Londri and I just stood there in the pool, staring at each other.

"What happened just now?" Londri asked.

I shrugged. "Well, they *do* seem to be a nice couple."

"Mmm. Just a little . . . *strange*."

"Well, of course, Londri. They are in love!"

Londri regarded me askance. "But I still think they were a little bit . . . *weird*. Don't you think so?"

"Come on, Londri. It's called *love*!" Then I added, "Someday it's going to happen to us, too, you know."

Londri's eyes opened wide as if he had just been hit by a premonition of things to come. He breathed deeply and sighed. "Yes. I know."

Then he looked at me, nodded, and smiled a mischievous smile.

◉ ◉ ◉

FIELD TRIPS

Father also took us out on field trips. We went strawberry picking, to a rodeo, a cave, a circus—and a very special performance: the Harlem Globetrotters. The circus was held in a gigantic tent. I don't have a full recollection of any of these trips, but I do remember some minor details. I will offer what comes to mind.

Strawberry picking meant getting down on your knees and advancing along rows and rows of the flowering shrub. Our knees, of course, would get all muddy and grubby. But what did we care? We were kids. We picked the strawberries with our hands and threw them into a small wooden basket. For every four or five we picked, we ate one. I consumed way too many. By the end of the day, my belly was so full that I thought it was going to explode.

That cured my urge to ever again go strawberry picking.

The rodeo—now, that sure was a treat! As we entered the bus on the way there, each child was given a shiny silver dollar—or maybe it was a half-dollar coin—plus some small change. We gaped at our newfound fortune with a chorus of "Ooh!"

At the rodeo we saw cowboys riding wild horses, bulls, and oxen. They would unfurl their lassos and twirl them around in huge circles and throw them at the feet of the bulls and oxen in order to rope them. The cowboys would then get off their horses and throw themselves on the animals to finish tying them up. They also had cowboy clowns to provide hilarious entertainment, and we laughed at their antics.

Of course, there were plenty of opportunities to spend the coins we had been given. Gift shops and food kiosks offering innumerable tempting delights claimed all of our cash—after all, we had no use for cash at the orphanage.

As far as the cave is concerned, I remember just a little bit about it. Once we entered the cave, we proceeded down an incline, which opened up into a large chamber. It was pitch black inside. A guide used a flashlight so that we could venture further inside. After walking for a little while, the guide suddenly turned the flashlight off, and we stopped, frozen, in that deep darkness. That part was scary. Some of the girls (and boys too) screeched in fear.

At that point, the guide, laughing loudly, turned on the flashlight again. He then directed our attention upward, and we beheld rock formations and ice crystals suspended from the ceiling. This was followed by another awed chorus from the children.

At the circus we saw pretty much what you would expect to see at a circus. There were plenty of jungle animals—elephants and leopards and chimps. And whenever a lion showed up, or a tiger or a bear, we would chant, as if on cue, the famous *Wizard of Oz* line: "Lions and tigers and bears! Oh my!"

And, of course, a circus could not possibly be a circus without clowns. We laughed heartily when an itty-bitty car entered the stage and circled it wildly several times before coming to a stop in the center. A door opened, and a clown stepped out of the diminutive automobile—followed by another clown, then another one and another. Clowns just kept exiting that tiny car, until a dozen or more had emerged. Then pandemonium broke out as they started running around the arena, whacking each other on the heads with colorful plastic baseball bats.

That, we thought, was really funny!

◉ ◉ ◉

LOS TROTAMUNDOS

One day, a group of the Cuban kids was discussing the dismal state of our basketball team as we stood under the water tower. We were speaking mostly in English, at times mixed with Spanish. For some of us, English was fast becoming our dominant language.

Marco expressed his disappointment. "I can't think of a worse team."

Gabe was more optimistic. "Our team has little guys. You have to remember that we are playing teams with big kids. Favian is our only good player, and he's a little guy!"

"That's true," Mateo chimed in. "But we should have won at least *one* game by now. Don't you think?"

Londri quipped, "*Los Trotamundos* we are not, that's for sure!"

"¿Los Trotamundos?" I inquired. "¿Qué es éso? What's that?"

Gabe explained. "In English you call them the Globetrotters."

"Okay, so," Marco insisted. "What is that?"

"Los Trotamundos are absolutely and without any doubt the best ever basketball team of all time in the whole wide world," Londri avowed

Gabe tried to explain. "Their full name is Globetrotters—the Harlem Globetrotters."

Domingo said, "They never lose."

"And we never win," Mateo added with a sad expression. "Our team must be the complete opposite of the—how do you call them? Glove what? Trappers?"

"Globe. Globetrotters," Domingo corrected him. "Yes, they are a great team, but they are funny, too!" he declared with a chuckle.

"They are known for some really amazing dribbling and for jumping real high to dunk a basketball!" Londri interjected with a wide grin. "It's like they can fly high up in the sky."

"They can spin a basketball on one finger," Gabe said. "They just keep spinning it and spinning it around—on their index finger!"

"And they run around the basketball court after a player from the other team," Londri went on, beaming, "with a bucket full of water, making believe they are mad at him, and when they throw it at him, he ducks, and the water goes all over the spectators! Except that it's not water. It's confetti. They are real funny!"

"And you know what? We are going to see them!" Gabe declared.

"What?" I asked. "When? Where?"

"Who cares where?" Gabe continued. "Somewhere! Soon!"

"How do you know that?" Mateo asked.

"I have connections." Gabe grinned, tapping his forehead with his index finger.

"Connections my foot!" Domingo said. "Father told the altar boys."

"How come I didn't hear him say that?" Mateo asked.

"Yeah," I added, "me either!"

"Because neither one of you was there," Domingo notified us.

We did go see the Harlem Globetrotters. Father took the whole orphanage. We needed two buses and, as usual, Father drove one of them.

Just as the guys had relayed, the Harlem Globetrotters were very funny. They demonstrated awesome dribbling, and when they went to dunk a basketball, they took such tall leaps that it looked like they could, as Londri had alleged, fly high up in the sky!

We recounted the highlights to one another later. "But the best part of all," I said, "was what Londri said, when they ran around the basketball court carrying a bucket of water to throw it at somebody from the other team."

"Yeah," Marco interrupted me, slapping his thigh with delight, "and when they threw it at him, it looked like he was gonna get wet, but it was confetti!"

Mateo said, "Stop saying *gonna*. The correct form is *going to*."

"Geez! Thank you for correcting my terrible grammar." Marco bowed and said, "Mr. Grammar Professor."

◉ ◉ ◉

THE BIG OAF

Riding back to the orphanage after one of these field trips, Norma and I sat together, as customary. I had a seat by the window.

Without warning, an eighth grader jumped in and sat next to Norma. He had to squeeze in tightly because it was a two-seater. Then he had the indolence to call her his *girlfriend!* Not only that, but he extended his arm over her shoulders and embraced her. I was beside myself. Norma was eight years old, for crying out loud! That's no age for a boyfriend.

To my dismay, Norma actually seemed pleased with the attention. I was shocked. My face grew hot with anger.

I shouted at him, "¡Déjala tranquila!" (Leave her alone!)

Even though he didn't speak Spanish, at the very least he had to appreciate that I was extremely annoyed. But he just laughed.

Remember when I said that I had learned not to mess with kids who were bigger than me? This time I didn't care and took a gamble. Risking my safety and security, I stood and pushed the big ruffian right off the seat. I showed him my fist and warned him, "Leave my sister alone or I'll beat you up, you big jerk!"

Yeah, right!

I braced for a retaliatory attack, but the big kid didn't say a word and took it in stride. He just smiled and sat in the rear of the bus, next to his chummy associates. They were all snickering. *Yeah, real funny!* Fortunately for me, the big oaf must have understood that I was defending my little sister. He could have pulverized me had he wanted to.

I stared at Norma reproachfully. Motioning with my face, I ordered her to sit by the window, as far away from that big lout as possible. Norma dropped her head in a sign of apology. Not a word was spoken.

She was silent for a very long time. We both were.

I was afraid that she wouldn't utter another word throughout the duration of the trip, so I told her, "You can talk if you want to, Norma."

She looked at me, crossed her arms, and looked away, saying, "But I don't want to!"

"Come on, Norma," I exclaimed. "For goodness sake, you're only eight years old!"

She turned to face me, crossed her arms tighter, then looked up and away from me again with a "Humph!"

I couldn't believe her tenacity.

"I don't want any hard feelings between us," I told her. "I was just looking out for you. That's all."

She just repeated the same sound: "Humph!"

After a few minutes, I quietly voiced my complaint. "So that's the kind of gratitude I get for coming to my sister's rescue."

Still looking away from me, she contended, "I know you were defending me against that bully. Thank you. I just didn't like you yelling at me."

"Norma," I reminded her, "I didn't raise my voice at all. I didn't even say a word."

She turned back to me. "You yelled at me with your eyes."

That shut me up again. *With my eyes.* I didn't know what to say.

After a minute or so, Norma said, "I'm glad you did it." And she smiled.

◉ ◉ ◉

BASKETBALL AND BOWLING

As I have mentioned before, we had a basketball team and a bowling league. When it came to basketball, the girls were our cheerleaders. They wore pleated skirts, twirled pom poms, and chanted the typical cheerleading songs: "Two, four, six, eight! Who do we appreciate? Saint Vincent's! Saint Vincent's! Saint Vincent's!"

However, their cheerleading was just for show, because we kept losing. We didn't have a terrible squad, considering that we didn't have eighth graders on the team and only two seventh graders. In spite of the losses, Favian carried the team on his shoulders, but we really couldn't expect him to do it all by himself. Besides Marshall, Favian had little support.

Our worse loss was by the score of sixty-three to seven (63-7!) against Saint John's, a team comprised of Goliaths. Our last game, against Saint Francis, was our best. We were actually leading by twenty to eighteen with less than a minute remaining in the game.

But more about that later.

Basketball is where my allegedly great memory really came into play. I remember every game, the name of every team we played, the score of every contest, and the color of the uniforms worn by the opponents. Rather than bore you with such minutiae, I decided to include these details in the back of the book in a section titled "Addendum".

Incidentally, our uniform consisted of red shorts and a white tank top with red piping. Each player's number was displayed in red on the reverse side of the tank top. I wore number eleven. I only played a few minutes in two games and never scored a point.

In all sincerity, I stunk.

Perhaps I'm being a little too hard on myself. I was practicing a lot, and my game was improving. The truth is that I had never played basketball in Cuba. I didn't even know the sport existed! Why Father chose to make me a member of the club in the first place was a mystery. Perhaps he was thinking of the future of the team and wanted me to get some experience. Basically, by the time I got to play, the team was in such disrepair that only a miracle would deliver even the slimmest of victories.

I never got a chance to demonstrate my new basketball skills because my stay at Saint Vincent's only lasted one year; before May 1963 rolled around, I was gone.

◉ ◉ ◉

BOWLING

Then there was bowling. We didn't play other schools, only against ourselves. Each dormitory had several teams, and each team had four or five kids. I wasn't very good at bowling. In the beginning, I got gutter ball after gutter ball and considered it a victory if I had fewer than three or four per game. The best score I ever had was a smidgen over one hundred. On one occasion, and only one occasion, was I able to bowl a whole game—*one* game—without throwing a gutter ball.

Norma, on the other hand, proved to be a great bowler. In one game she kept throwing strike after strike. She was the best bowler not only among girls her age but also among all of the girls at Saint Vincent's. In fact, she was a much better bowler than most of the boys. Her best score was over two hundred.

Boys and girls did not compete against each other, though. That was truly unfortunate because I never saw her play. Norma was declared a champion bowler and won three trophies.

Good old Normita!

◉ ◉ ◉

EXEMPLARY LIVES

My mother sent me frequent packages containing *Vidas Ejemplares*—"Exemplary Lives"—at a considerable cost to herself because she knew that I loved reading them. These were the life stories of virtuous people told in comic-book fashion as a way to familiarize children with the lives of saints and were very popular in Cuba. Each comic book was composed of thirty-two colorful pages drawn in beautiful detail. Some of the other kids were curious and asked to read them. I was glad to share them, provided that they were returned.

My mom also sent me *Vidas Ilustres*—"Illustrious Lives." As with *Vidas Ejemplares*, these were thirty-two colorful pages, in comic-book format, depicting renowned and venerated personalities who, by the lives they had lived, had played a significant role in society. I particularly enjoyed reading about Thomas Alva Edison and Albert Einstein.

Unfortunately, one day, I found a whole bunch of these comic books ripped up, in the garbage. None of the kids who had borrowed them admitted to doing such a thing. I decided to ask Sister Cordelia if she knew anything about it.

"I threw them away," she acknowledged.

"But why?" I wanted to know.

"They were scattered all over the table in the rec room and on the floor, as if they were rubbish. If you consider those comic books to be trash, Antonio, they belong in the garbage. You left a mess in the rec room."

"Not me, Sister. I never leave my things lying all over the place in the rec room."

"Who, then?" Basically, she was accusing me. "You must learn to be more orderly, Antonio."

"I let some of the guys read them, Sister, but they always give them back to me."

"They were left in disarray, as if you no longer cared for them. You must learn to take stock of your possessions, young man."

That was the end of that discussion. I felt betrayed by Sister Cordelia, and it took me a while to simmer down. Deep down, I felt that one of the guys was responsible; I just didn't know who. At any rate, the experience taught me to be more careful about lending my things to others.

◉ ◉ ◉

THE TELEPHONE CALL

The nuns found me on the playground by the picnic tables, playing with Londri and some of the other guys. "Your mother is on the phone!" one told me.

I ran inside to find Norma already waiting for me by the phone in the hallway.

I picked up the telephone and covered the receiver with the palm of my hand. Turning to Norma, I quietly cautioned her—as Gabe had once cautioned the boys from D6—"Be careful what you say, Norma." I was whispering. "Don't compromise Mom. For her safety, assume that the Communists are listening. And let me assure you, they *are* listening."

I spoke into the receiver. "Is that you, Mom?"

Our mother had called to give us news. "Benny and I just got married!"

Our first reaction was one of shock. Though we knew Benny rather well, we had no clue that this would happen. He was a member of our group of church people who would do things together. Actually, his name was Benito; Benny was his nickname.

Our group comprised about ten of us, sometimes more. We would go to restaurants and to the movies. We would also go to the park and on picnics, singing songs and playing guessing games like charades. A couple of times, Benny took the three of us (Mom, Norma, and me) to a Chinese restaurant. As a matter of fact, we spent New Year's Eve with him in a Chinese restaurant to welcome 1962. He also took us to his home, where he lived with his parents, his sister, and her teenage daughter.

Well, evidently, Benny and Mom had been dating all along! We were just so young that we didn't put two and two together.

When our mom gave us the news, Norma and I voiced our approval. Our mom sounded very happy, and we were happy for her.

Benny also got on the telephone with us and asked, "Is it okay with you that I am your dad now?"

"Of course it is!" we both replied enthusiastically.

"We would have a complete family again!" I remember saying.

"We will all soon be reunited in the United States," our mom told us.

Ah. That word *soon* was a tricky one! What does *soon* really mean?

At any rate, the four of us would be together in the foreseeable future, whenever that would be. Mom told us that she would probably come to the United States first, and then Benny would follow. That was the plan. That was the part that had to be worked out; there was a little glitch. Benny was what Fidel called a counterrevolutionary. We didn't know to what extent, but he had been jailed a couple times. According to the grapevine, he got caught stapling anti-Communist flyers on telephone poles and bus stop bulletin boards.

But for now, he was free, and our mom was free. Well, as free as anyone could ever be in a police state.

○ ○ ○

STOP THE CAR!

Learning about our mom's marriage to Benny and realizing that we would have a new dad brought me a memory of our real dad.

Papi and I were in the car together, driving on the highway—just the two of us. I was probably about three years old. It was getting dark, and we were approaching a railroad track. The alarm started ringing its warning. Cars sped by, trying to beat the yellow traffic light before it turned red. My dad put his foot to the pedal. He also wanted to beat the traffic light.

"No, Daddy! Stop!" I yelled.

"Don't worry, son," my dad said. "I'll be able to cross the tracks before the light turns red."

I let out a loud shriek. "Stop the car, Daddy!" I was panic stricken. "Stop the car now! Please, Daddy!"

"Okay, son." My dad could see that I was petrified and slowly came to a stop. Other cars continued to speed by. The car behind us started honking. Its driver wanted us to proceed, but my dad held his ground.

"Don't pay attention to the guy behind us," he said, looking in his rearview mirror. "I'm not going to let that bald-headed guy with the bushy mustache drive our car."

The railroad crossing arm came down with an earsplitting warning signal. I slumped down on the floor of the car and curled myself into a fetal position. The driver behind us was beside himself, honking repeatedly. I closed my eyes and put my fingers in my ears to block out the piercing blare.

"Remember what I just said." My dad peered down at me on the floor. "Don't worry about the guy behind us. I'll never let him drive our car."

Once the train had passed, the railroad arm was raised. It only took a few minutes, but it had seemed like an eternity. My father drove for a block and turned a corner. He shut the ignition off, got out of the car, and went to the passenger side where I lay, still slumped down on the floor. He opened the door, lifted me into his arms, and embraced me. He reassured me, "Don't you worry, son, I'll protect you!"

He walked in the direction of the train track and pointed to the railroad arm. "See," he said, "it's up there now. We are safe. *You* are safe, my dear little one. I got you."

Then, holding me tight and close to his heart, he walked back to the car and whispered, as he had done many other times, "Patica, ¿paqué te quiero?"

When we got to the car, he looked me directly in the eyes and declared, "Tony, my son, you are my most precious child." He kissed me on the forehead and on my cheeks. "I love you with all my heart. Nothing can ever—nothing *will* ever—come between us!"

He opened the passenger door and sat me down on the seat. Climbing back behind the wheel, he turned on the engine, and we drove off into the night, safe and sound.

"I love you, Daddy," I said.

"I love you too, son."

A year later, leukemia would claim his life.

CHAPTER IX

Autumn

Autumn arrived, and with it regular classes, bowling, and basketball. A few new Cuban children entered the orphanage and a few departed. Unfortunately, Gabe was gone, and so was Domingo. There were no goodbyes.

Sister Cordelia was now permanently in charge of D6. She also became our classroom teacher. Sister Kevin was a hard act to follow, but Sister Cordelia had a nice personality and truly cared for us. Slowly, she earned our respect and esteem. I even forgave her for ripping up and throwing away my comic books. I figured that I was partly to blame.

I have no recollection of actual classroom lessons, but I vaguely remember Sister Cordelia trying to teach arithmetic by way of currency. I will try to reenact one such lesson.

She would ask the class, "If you buy a loaf of bread that costs two dimes and a penny, and you pay for it with a quarter, how much money will you get back?"

Many hands were raised. These children knew the answer—four cents. However, some did not know the value of money because they had never handled pocket change.

Sister would probe further by asking similar questions—for example, "How much are two dimes?" "How much is a quarter and a nickel?" "What about a quarter, a dime, and a penny?" Inevitably, she would get the same result—many hands would be raised; some would not.

Sister soon tailored her lessons to address this issue. I think she also offered these youngsters additional support after class. We had evening classes a couple times a week. This gave us a chance to do our homework and receive extra help.

Sister Cordelia also taught us practical things, like how to sew and darn our socks. Sometimes we drew pictures or sang songs—especially during the holidays. We also read children's magazines. I particularly liked *Boys' Life*, the monthly magazine of the Boy Scouts of America. I found some of the stories there fascinating. I learned a lot of English from them and, believe it or not, by reading the jokes.

There's a particular joke I'll never forget. It had to do with a disagreement between two persons. It went like this: the first one says, "I didn't come here to get offended!" The second one replies, "Where do you usually go?"

When I first read it, I found it so funny that I laughed out loud. The kids sitting near me noticed my enjoyment, as did Sister Cordelia. She came over to me and remarked, "You understood that joke, Antonio. That's wonderful! Comprehending jokes in English is a sign that you're really learning the language." Then she added, "Dreaming in English, well, that's proof in the pudding that you are really mastering your new language!"

Grasping the meaning of *proof in the pudding* was another sign that I was, indeed, mastering my new language. But I couldn't help thinking, *What a weird expression!*

Once, during one of our evening classes, I meandered over to Sister Cordelia, intrigued by a framed photograph of a handsome family on her desk. The lady in the picture was beautiful and wore a stylish pink dress. The gentleman—I assumed that he was the lady's husband—wore a dark-gray suit with a white shirt and blue tie. Two small children sat on their laps, a girl and her little brother.

"Do you know who they are, Antonio?" Sister asked me.

I shrugged.

"That's the president of the United States, John Fitzgerald Kennedy, and his lovely wife, Jacqueline. We call them Jack and Jackie. The little girl's name is Caroline, and her little brother has the same name as his father, John."

"The president and his family?" I was intrigued. I couldn't remember ever having seen their photographs.

Sister Cordelia added, with pride in her voice, "President Kennedy is Roman Catholic! He's the first Catholic president of our nation!"

◎ ◎ ◎

BASKETBALL

The basketball season began in earnest in early autumn. As I stated earlier, Father was our coach, and Favian was our star athlete. Marshall was our second-best player, but he was not in Favian's league. The rest of the guys played decent basketball, but their height was no match for the tall guys on the other teams. We were told that last year's team had been pretty good, finishing the season in third place. But most of those players were eighth graders and were no longer on our team. They had graduated from the orphanage.

How Favian weathered the season is beyond me. His patience and determination was a testament to his character.

Our first game was against Saint John's. They got on the basketball court before the game to take practice shots at the same time as our team did.

Londri and I were sitting in the bleachers. We were shocked when we saw Saint John's players. Londri exclaimed, "Look at the size of those guys!"

"Oh my God!" I exclaimed. "Well"—I tried to put a good spin on it—"I do like their red uniforms. They match our red-and-white outfit."

"Uniforms don't win games, Antonio!"

Our cheerleaders were also amazed when they took a look at the opposing team.

"Holy moly!" one of them yelped as she turned to her companion.

"They are giants," exclaimed her friend.

Favian, who was practicing layups, overheard their remarks. "Height doesn't matter," he countered. "We have a good team, and we're going to win."

Favian turned to Marshall, who was practicing layups with him. "Right, Marshall?"

Marshall took a good look at Saint John's titans, scratched his head, and answered, not too convincingly, "Yeah, we're gonna win, all right. I guess. Maybe."

"You don't sound believable, Marshall," retorted a cheerleader.

"Where's your resolve, Marshall?" Favian admonished him. "You have to have faith!"

Marshall just shook his shoulders. His foreboding proved correct. Saint John's won easily, forty-eight to twenty-eight.

Our next game was against another team of giants. As always, I tried to put a good spin on it. "They have nice uniforms."

"I told you that uniforms don't win games, Antonio!"

"Still, I do like their uniform—all black."

Saint Lawrence beat us into submission by thirty-two to ten.

⊙ ⊙ ⊙

MR. MCCARTHY

Mr. McCarthy lived in the town of Vincennes and visited the orphanage from time to time. He would alternate taking ten to twelve of us boys out into the woods to teach us about various animals we would encounter there, as well as insects and plants. Once or twice he brought his two sons with him, who were our age. They spent a couple of days with us and slept in our dormitory.

Mr. McCarthy was especially wary of poison ivy and showed us how to identify it and avoid it. "It grows in clusters of three leaflets," he told us. "So, remember this: leaves of three, let it be." He also taught us how to smoke. Well, he tried, anyway, by demonstrating how to cut a reed and light it. This, naturally, was before society in general was made aware of the danger of smoking.

"You don't have to spend money on fancy cigarettes," he told us. "You can smoke for free." He picked a reed, snapped it off the stem with a switchblade, and showed us the reed was hollow inside. Searching in his pocket for a cigarette lighter, he ignited the reed. He took a few puffs and gave it to one of his sons to take a few puffs.

"See how easy it is?"

That son passed the reed on to his brother, who took a few puffs and handed it to one of the orphanage kids. That kid took a puff and began to cough.

Mr. McCarthy advised, "Don't inhale so quick. Just take a puff and let it out gently."

"Watch me," said one of the McCarthy boys. "All you have to do is inhale, take it in for a bit, and let it go out real slow." He demonstrated, saying, "Like my dad said, see how easy it is?"

He gave the reed to another boy, who inhaled and exhaled without a hitch. That boy, in turn, passed it on to another one, and so on. After a while, the reed had been passed along to most of us. Only a couple of kids inhaled and exhaled with no problem, but for the majority there was a lot of coughing and hacking. Two or three of us didn't want anything to do with that reed and refused to smoke it. I was one of those.

One of the boys asked, "If you don't have a cigarette lighter, can you use matches?"

"Yes, you can," Mr. McCarthy said, "but I'll tell you what . . ."

Mr. McCarthy was always saying "I'll tell you what."

He searched in his pocket again and took out a magnifying glass and a piece of paper. "Watch this," he said. He crumpled the paper, placed it on the ground, and held the magnifying glass between the sun and the paper. He tilted the magnifying glass back and forth until a small dot came into view. In about thirty seconds, a flame materialized. This was followed by a chorus of "Wow!" from the kids.

The same kid asked, "What if there is no sun, or it's dark?"

"Well, in that case you can start a fire with sticks," Mr. McCarthy stated, "but you have to be real patient 'cause it takes a long time."

"We got plenty of sticks here," another boy added, "and we got plenty of time."

"Ah, a wise guy!" Mr. McCarthy grinned. "I'll tell you what: we'll leave that demonstration for another day."

"Aw!"

"Don't be disappointed," Mr. McCarthy said. "I've got a surprise for you."

"A surprise?"

"Today I wanted to talk about what you can do when you're out in the woods. One thing is smoking." He took a puff of the reed. "Another thing is camping. And guess what, boys? We're going camping . . . soon!"

"Yay!"

"I've spoken to Mother Superior, and she has given us permission. First thing we need to do is get our gear together. Now, some people may say you need a tent and a sleeping bag. Nah, I'm gonna show you how to camp out in the rough, and you're gonna love it!" Then he added, "I'll tell you what, though, when you're out in the woods, watch out for poison ivy . . . and wolves!"

I think that Mr. McCarthy loved to scare us.

◉ ◉ ◉

ANOTHER PHONE CALL

Sister Cordelia found me playing checkers with Londri in the rec room and told me that my mom was on the phone. I rushed down to the first-floor telephone booth. Norma was on the phone.

"Mom's here!" Norma was excited. "She's here, in the United States!"

"What?" I wasn't sure I had heard correctly. "How?"

"How should I know?" Norma shrugged. "Pan Am, I guess." Then she handed me the phone. "Talk to her."

Mom told me that she had just landed in Miami and was staying temporarily with Graciela, an old friend, in her apartment. Mom said that she would start looking for a job and get her own place so that we could join her.

"How about Benny?" I asked.

"His visa has not yet been approved, but he should be coming soon."

"Really?" The thought of having a full family was exciting, but persistent questions begged for an answer. "When? How soon?"

"Real soon," my mom said. "I don't know, Tony. You know how these things are. I'm doing my best."

"Well . . " I tried to sound optimistic. "That's great!"

Nonetheless, I couldn't help thinking that it was quite possible Benny had been taken prisoner by the Communists for participating in anti-revolutionary activities. I realized that his journey to the United States could be fraught with difficulties.

That night, while lying in bed, my thoughts took me back to my dad. It was my second birthday party, and the whole family had come to my grandparents' house. We gathered together in the dining room around a big birthday cake on the table.

Tía Elvira said, "Blow out the candles, Tony!"

Somebody had a camera and was about to take my picture. I don't know what got into me, but I didn't want my picture taken. I dropped down on the floor and crawled under the table.

One of my cousins shouted, "Oh, come on, Tony! Stop being such a baby!"

What? Is he kidding? I am *a baby!*

Another cousin got down on her knees, grabbed one of my legs, and dragged me out from under the table. I stood and looked at her, then at everybody. The man with the camera got ready to take my picture again, and I hightailed it out of there. I ran into my grandparents' bedroom and slid under the bed.

My dad chased me into the bedroom and peeked under the bed. "Come on, son," he said. "It's just a picture. It's not going to hurt."

"No!" I yelled. "I don't wanna!"

I decided to be stubborn. I don't remember what else happened, but it's obvious that some pictures were actually taken, because I have them in my possession.

◉ ◉ ◉

CAMPING OUT

The day of the camping expedition finally arrived. We were all excited as we gathered outside on the basketball court. Mr. McCarthy had selected twelve D6 boys for the first excursion, and I was fortunate to be among them. He and his sons were wearing backpacks. One of his sons held two large coolers.

"I was only kidding about not needing sleeping bags, boys," he said. "Yep, me and my sons do use sleeping bags whenever we go camping. By the way"—he smiled—"Mother Superior used her power of persuasion on the townsfolk, and they donated these." He pointed to several hefty bundles on the ground. "Twelve brand-new backpacks, each with a spanking-new sleeping bag inside!"

Our mouths hung open in amazement.

"The sleeping bags are lightweight, like you are." We all laughed. "That way those suckers fit real snug inside the backpacks. Go ahead now and pick one up for yourself! Like I said, me and my boys have our own."

We pounced on those precious bundles like there was no tomorrow.

"Wait a doggone minute, now!" He was taken aback by our ravenous behavior. "Listen up, now! Just so there are no misunderstandings, this gear ain't yours to keep. The twelve kids who come camping with me next time will use 'em, then the next twelve after that will use 'em, and so on. Let's just call 'em *loaners*. Do you understand?"

"Yes, sir," we all replied.

"Good. Go on then, pick one up for yourself and follow me."

Each of us grabbed a backpack and peeked inside. Yes, there was a sleeping bag in there all right! We strapped our backpacks on and proceeded to follow Mr. McCarthy into the woods. We hiked for a while, stopping every so often as Mr. McCarthy pointed to the foliage and animals scurrying about, teaching us about them. Eventually, we came to a spot he liked.

"This is our home for the night, boys. Dump your backpacks, and let's go fetch us some firewood. We're gonna clear a small area right here and fill it with a whole bunch of kindling."

Mr. McCarthy showed us how to prepare the ground for a campfire. We did as he instructed and built a small, triangular tower of sticks and twigs.

"Oh, heck, I forgot my matches!" Mr. McCarthy exclaimed. "Now, how in the world are we ever gonna get a fire started?" He laughed. "I'll tell you what: we're going to do it the way the Indians did it. All we need are two dry sticks and some dry moss. Just make sure they are dry."

He looked around him, grabbed some dry, brown moss lying at the base of a tree, and selected two sticks that were about two feet long. The thicker one was about three inches in diameter, the thinner one half that size.

"All ya gotta do is take the big stick, split it down the middle, carve a little canal along its length, and start rubbing it with the other stick to start a fire. But first you gotta do this."

He searched in his backpack and took out an axe and a large knife. He stood the thicker stick on an old tree stump, struck it with the axe three or four times, and chopped it open right down the middle. He took one of the halves and laid on the dirt, bark-side down. Positioning his knee on one end of it so that it wouldn't move too much, he started to carve a groove along its length with the knife, fashioning a canal. It took a while to do this. When this task was completed, he took the thinner stick and sharpened one end with the knife. He started rubbing the sharpened end rapidly up and down along the canal he had carved on the thicker stick.

"Make sure the smaller stick has a sharp end, and just keep rubbing

". . . fast." He kept rubbing and rubbing. "It doesn't happen right away." He was breathing hard. "Gotta be patient."

In a short time, a small stream of smoke started to emerge from the stick. "Yep, it's smoking, but it ain't ready yet. Just keep on rubbing a little bit longer."

After a few seconds, there was a lot of smoke. He stopped rubbing and pointed to a smoldering black residue that had formed at the base of the stick.

"See that patch that looks like black ash?" He paused to catch his breath. "Yep, it's smoking all right!" He waved the brown moss he had picked up earlier. "Well, let's scoop that smoldering black residue right up and dump it into this here brown moss."

He flung the smoldering ash into the center of the brown moss and folded the moss over the ash. Blowing some air into it, he waved it around. The moss started to burn. He brought it over to the kindling that we had built up and tossed the burning moss in. And before you knew it, fire!

We all cried out, "Wow!" Our mouths were wide open in astonishment.

"Like I said"—he was still out of breath—"ya gotta be patient 'cause it takes a while." He dried his forehead with his arm. "But it works!" He inhaled deeply. "Whew! I'll tell you what, it's quite a workout!"

He paused, looked at us, and said, "Heck, that's way too complicated and time-consuming, ain't it? Thank goodness we live in the twentieth century!" He took out his cigarette lighter and showed it to us, snickering. "In a pinch, just use this."

The kids laughed.

Then he took out a book of matches from his pocket. "You can use these too."

One of the kids said, "You said you had no matches!"

Mr. McCarthy grinned mischievously and replied, "I lied."

The kids laughed again.

Mr. McCarthy opened his backpack. "Tell you what, time for some chow; whatta ya say?" He took out a few cans of pork and beans, tuna fish, and sardines.

One of the boys exclaimed excitedly, "Oh boy, sardines!" He paused, gave Mr. McCarthy a solemn look, and added, "Yuck!"

Another boy repeated the same sentiments.

Mr. McCarthy took it in stride. "Well, I'll tell you what . . ." He smiled. "Some of us love sardines!"

A third boy also expressed the same opinion: "Yuck!"

"The less you have, the more we have."

His sons then opened the coolers to show us various sandwiches and soda bottles. One of them said, "We have ham sandwiches, turkey sandwiches, cheese sandwiches, peanut butter and jelly."

The first sardine hater said, "Well, that's more like it!"

"I'm glad you approve, kid!" Mr. McCarthy said. "But first, let's go see what the woods have to offer."

He took us into the woods and showed us how to gather berries. Later that afternoon, we built a campfire and ate from our bounty.

When we had finished our meal, he exclaimed, "Wait a minute! You can't have a campfire without dessert!" He reached into his backpack and took out a few bags of marshmallows. "I'll tell you what, let's fetch us some long, razor-sharp sticks."

We scurried into the bushes and picked a few thin, pointed twigs to poke through the marshmallows. We roasted the confections over the campfire as nightfall set upon us.

"Now, I know that you don't really believe in ghosts," he said slowly. "Right?" Then he added, "Nah, of course you don't. I gotta warn you, though . . . watch out for wolves!"

He regaled us that night with ghost stories. I don't remember the stories, simply because I didn't believe in ghosts. I don't think too many of us did—although I wondered. Still, being out in the woods at night made us rethink our theories about the existence of ghosts. What with ghosts and wolves and it being pitch black and all, it got downright scary! Mr. McCarthy talked and talked, until our eyes got so heavy that we couldn't keep them open any longer.

Mr. McCarthy noticed that we were falling asleep. "I think it's time to slide into our sleeping bags, boys, and hit the hay." It didn't take me long to fall asleep.

◉ ◉ ◉

MISSILE CRISIS

On October 16, 1962, we watched President Kennedy on television as he addressed the nation about the ominous confrontation between the United States and the Soviet Union in what became known as the Missile Crisis. It lasted from October 16 through 28 that year and was instigated by the discovery of Soviet ballistic deployment in Cuba.

The thirteen-day confrontation has often been considered the closest the world has ever come to a full-scale nuclear war and mutually assured destruction, known by its initials: MAD.

By then I spoke English rather well, almost fluently—for a kid, that is. President Kennedy was on TV using grown-up and technological English. I didn't understand the full implications of what he was talking about. I started to applaud, thinking that Kennedy had said that the United States was going to invade Cuba again and drive Fidel out of power. A year and a half earlier, from April 17 through 20, 1961, the Bay of Pigs had proven unsuccessful in deposing Fidel Castro.

One of the older kids came to me and asked, "Do you understand what the president just said?"

"Yes," I replied, "he's going to kick Fidel out of Cuba!"

"No, Antonio, what he said is that Russia has nuclear bombs in Cuba. This is a very dangerous situation. Do you understand?"

"Nuclear bombs?" I asked incredulously. "In Cuba?" *Oh boy, do I understand now!*

Incidentally, this was when Operation Pedro Pan came to a dead stop, though a few children who had come to the US earlier still came to

Saint Vincent's Orphanage, and other Cubans continued to trickle into the country—not only children, but adults as well. The real possibility of a full-scale nuclear war and mutually assured destruction kept me awake at night, especially because it implicated Cuba.

⊙ ⊙ ⊙

PROWLERS LURKING IN THE NIGHT

Something woke me up in the middle of the night. We had gone camping. I was certain that I had heard a noise.

Yes, there it is again. Indeed, something, or someone, was stirring in the woods. It was quite dark, but I clearly saw a pair of eyes in the bushes, burning brightly and blinking, staring right at us! As I scanned the area, I spotted more pairs of eyes spying on us.

The pairs of eyes got closer and closer, and suddenly the most petrifying howl I had ever heard pierced the night!

"Wolves!" cried Mr. McCarthy. "Run for your lives, boys!"

Every boy tore out of his sleeping bag and fled, but my zipper got stuck. I tried and I tried, but I just couldn't break loose. Panic engulfed me.

Before I knew it, a wolf was standing right above me, staring down at me with shiny, blood-stained yellow teeth that looked like sharp spears, threatening and hungry, saliva dripping out of its mouth.

"Help! Help!" I screamed.

Someone was holding me by the shoulders, shaking me. "Are you okay?"

It was Londri. I was in the orphanage, sitting up on my bed.

"I think you were having a nightmare, Antonio."

I tried shaking the cobwebs out of my head. "Wow," I said, "I'm so glad it was just a dream. It seemed so real!"

My screams woke up a few boys. "I'm sorry, guys," I apologized. "Everything's fine. Go back to sleep."

◉ ◉ ◉

BASKETBALL WOES

The basketball schedule called for a double-header against a team by the name of Saint Joseph's. The bus ride was long and arduous. The first game was played by a squad made up of fourth and fifth graders. The second game was composed of sixth through eighth graders. As before, Londri and I watched the games from the bleachers.

"This team's uniform is not attractive at all," I complained to Londri. "It's an ugly gray, and the top is not a basketball tank top at all. It's a T-shirt with short sleeves."

"You're right," Londri agreed. "I've never seen a basketball team wearing a T-shirt with sleeves."

And as had become customary, we lost both games. We little kids lost the first one by a score of fifteen to five. The tally for the second game was twenty-eight to thirteen.

◉ ◉ ◉

JUST A PLAIN OLD BULLY

So, I had learned never to mess with kids who were bigger than me—but what about when a bigger kid messed with me?

Well, let me tell you about an incident that occurred in the shower room.

Wyatt was in a really foul mood that day. He was always in a foul mood, but on this particular day he was especially angry. He just kept pushing me—in the chapel, in the refectory, in the hallway—all day. He never needed an excuse. He was just a plain old bully, always picking on the little kids.

We were in the lavatory. I was wearing my bathrobe because I had just taken a shower and was on my way to brush my teeth and comb my hair when Wyatt pushed me hard against the sink.

"Stop it, Wyatt!" I said to him.

"Whatcha gonna do about it?"

"I'm going to push you back, that's what!" So I pushed him.

Wyatt's eyes opened wide with anger. "Oh, so you wanna play, eh?" And he pushed me again.

"Stop it, Wyatt." I repeated. "You are such a dope . . . and so stupid."

"Oh yeah?" Calling Wyatt a dope was bad enough, but I had just called him stupid. He whispered, "Who you calling stupid?" Lowering his voice made him sound really scary.

I was terrified, but I found the courage to affirm what I thought of him. "You! I'm calling *you* stupid!"

At twelve years of age, Wyatt was not only two years my senior, he was also much taller and stronger. He slapped my face twice, picked me up under my arms, and violently dragged me all the way to the wall. He grabbed me by the neck with his left arm and pinned me, holding me against the wall. Then he started punching me in the face with his right fist, knocking my glasses onto the floor. I tried punching back, throwing jabs at his face, but my arms were too short and couldn't reach him.

Londri, Favian, and Marshall, who also were in the lavatory brushing their teeth, came running to my rescue. Favian yelled at his brother, "Let him go, Wyatt!" Favian and Marshall gripped Wyatt by his arms and broke us apart. I sank to the floor, blood oozing out of my nose.

I felt that Wyatt shouldn't be allowed to get away with bullying. He had to be stopped. I sensed an opportunity, sprang on him, and clasped his arms tightly by his waist. Then I rammed my right knee into his groin as powerfully as I could—four, five, six times—and shoved him. Wyatt fell backwards over Londri, who had gotten down on his knees to retrieve my glasses. Wyatt hit the back of his head against the floor, hard. He yelped in agony.

"Serves you right for starting a fight!" Favian admonished his brother.

"You had it coming," Londri stated.

"You sure did!" Marshall added. "Why don't you pick on somebody your own size, anyway?"

"I apologize for Wyatt, Antonio," Favian told me. "He's my brother, but he's a jerk!"

Sister Cordelia came running. "What's going on?"

Londri stealthily gave me a towel to wipe my bloody face and stood in front of me, trying to shield me from Sister Cordelia's view.

"Nothing's going on, Sister," Favian answered. "We were just playing."

"Yeah," Marshall declared. "Everything's just fine."

"Don't hide him." Sister Cordelia waved Londri away so that she could get a good look at my face. Then she confirmed the obvious: "You're bleeding, Antonio!"

"I'm okay, Sister, really. Like Favian said, we were just playing a game."

"That's right. It's just a game," Londri asserted.

"Come on, Sister," Marshall added, "you know how boys are! We play rough. Ha ha!"

"Well," she sighed. "So long as nobody gets killed." As she was exiting the bathroom area, she said, "Wash his face, Favian."

Sister Cordelia observed Wyatt, who was kneeling on the floor now, rubbing the back of his head, whimpering and humiliated.

"You look like a vanquished bully, Wyatt," she said to him. "I hope you learned your lesson."

Suddenly, I felt sorry for the nuns—always having to put out fires.

Anyhow, that's how I learned never to let kids who were bigger than me mess with me.

Word got around the orphanage that "Wyatt got beat up real bad" and I was the one who did it. All of a sudden, the kids started looking up to me. I had earned a small measure of respect. I was a celebrity! And all I did was give him a little push.

I had to admit, it felt good.

Another positive outcome of this fight is that I realized I could now see without glasses. I no longer needed them.

◎ ◎ ◎

MELODY

That evening after my fight with Wyatt, as we entered the refectory for supper, I caught Melody looking at me with those adoring eyes of hers. My eyes and hers locked. I smiled, thinking, *Boy, she is a real beauty!*

Suddenly, I became dreadfully aware of the unspoken rule: boys are not supposed to like girls! I looked away quickly, warm with embarrassment.

As usual, Norma caught this interaction between Melody and me and grinned softly. Kieran, who was a wise guy, also caught the interaction. He turned to me, teasing in a singsong way, "Antonio has a girlfriend!"

I shook my head as I pondered my situation. *How do I counter Kieran's insinuation? What can I say?*

"No, I don't have a girlfriend!" was the best I could muster.

Kieran continued the singsong: "Antonio has a girlfriend!"

I could have protested until the chickens came home to roost.

"Stop it, Kieran!"

Londri, who was sitting next to me, did not look happy. The other boys at our table lowered their eyes, sly smiles crossing their lips. I glanced over at the table where Favian and Marshall were sitting. They did not look very happy, either. But as far as I could tell, I had given Melody no encouragement.

Wait a minute! I did smile at her!

The boys at my table picked up Kieran's ludicrous chant: "Antonio has a girlfriend!" And they added, "Nyah-nyah, nyah nyah-nyah!"

"I do not have a girlfriend!" I insisted. Acting quickly to divert attention, I impulsively marched over to Wyatt's table and stood right in front of him. He gazed at me, startled. I held out my right hand in a show of reconciliation. He looked at it for a few seconds, dumbfounded, trying to figure out whether to accept it. Then he extended his, and we shook hands. The boys at his table clapped and patted us on the back cheerfully.

From that day on, Wyatt never gave me any particular trouble.

On my way back to my table, I could not help but glance over at Melody. She sure was pretty, and her name was undeniably music to my ears.

True to his nature, Wyatt kept on blaming the Cubans whenever something went wrong—like the time someone broke a lamp in the rec room, and when someone threw several rolls of bathroom tissue in the lavatory toilets. In those instances, Wyatt's accusatory "*Cubans!*" battle cry was alive and well.

Well, habits don't die overnight. Some simmer and persist.

◎ ◎ ◎

ORPHANS AND REFUGEES

A few days later, a group of us were getting ready to play basketball in the outdoor court. Favian and Marshall were the captains of the two teams. Londri, Kieran, and Marco were on Favian's team—they had four guys. I was on Marshall's team along with Mateo, who was Marco's brother, which made it a crew of three. We needed one more.

So, guess who else played? None other than Wyatt himself. It was beyond my understanding. I wasn't too keen on the idea, but there he was, on the court with the rest of us—as my teammate!

Here's what happened: Favian and Marshall had concocted a plan. They felt that playing on the same squad would give Wyatt and me an opportunity to further settle our differences.

Favian addressed us, "Antonio, Wyatt, dear brother of mine, we think it's a good idea for the two of you to play on the same team."

"What? Why?" Apparently, Wyatt wasn't too keen on the idea, either.

"Me and Favian, we discussed it," Marshall answered.

"Yes," Favian added, "we figured it might help you two iron things out."

Wyatt let out a little bit of steam. "We ain't got nothing to iron out!"

Favian and Marshall grabbed Wyatt and me by the shoulders and positioned us face-to-face, but we both stared at the ground.

"Look each other in the eye!" Marshall commanded.

Abiding by Marshall's order, we glanced at each other. I extended my hand to Wyatt as I had the other day, but this time he refused to shake it. I wasn't sure what else to do, so I smiled. Wyatt did not smile.

"Come on, shake hands!" Favian instructed.

Wyatt observed me for a few seconds, then shook my hand, albeit reluctantly.

"Okay!" Marshall hollered—rather hurriedly, probably fearing that Wyatt might change his mind. "Let's play ball!"

So we played ball. Everything was working smoothly for five minutes or so until Wyatt hit Marco on the hand as he was going for a layup. Wyatt didn't do it deliberately; he was just trying to block a shot.

"Foul!" Marco and Favian shouted in unison.

"Whatta ya talking about?" Wyatt roared angrily. "That was no foul!"

"Yes, it was, Wyatt," Marshall countered. "You hit Marco."

"I didn't hit 'im!" Wyatt replied. "It was a clean block."

"Oh, come on, Wyatt," Favian said, "you did too hit 'im."

"Oh yeah? Wanna do something about it?" Wyatt walked straight up to Favian and tried to intimidate him, glowering at him two inches from his face. "I don't care if you are my brother!"

"Come on, Wyatt," Favian said. "Stop."

"No!" Wyatt yelled and pushed him. "You stop!"

Favian pushed Wyatt back, and Wyatt grabbed him by his jersey collar. Wyatt was stronger and a couple of inches taller than his younger brother. Marshall and Londri ran to intervene and separated them.

"This is ridiculous!" Wyatt screamed at the top of his lungs. "I don't wanna play this stupid game anymore!" And he stomped away.

We watched him leave. He went inside the building and slammed the door behind him. We were all quiet. No one had the courage to say anything out of respect for Favian.

As Favian's best friend, Marshall broke the silence. No one else would dare speak. He tried to make light of it.

"Hey, Favian," he probed, smiling, "you sure he's your brother?"

Favian looked seriously at Marshall. "To tell you God's honest truth, I'm not rightly sure that he is."

"Really?" Marshall was startled. "You are not sure?"

"We never wanted to talk about it," Favian divulged, "but my mom told me that when Wyatt was a little baby, somebody left him outside the front door in a picnic basket."

We all looked at each other incredulously.

"It's a family secret."

Favian tried to keep a serious demeanor but couldn't. A slight grin crossed his lips, and he broke out laughing. After a few startled seconds, we were laughing along with him.

"Why is he so angry all the time?" I ventured to ask. "You are not at all like him."

Favian shrugged. "You got me."

"Do you have any other brothers and sisters like him?" Kieran asked.

"Truth is, I don't know if I have any other brothers and sisters," Favian said. "I don't even know anything about my dad. All I know is that I have a mom." Favian shook his head. "Used to, anyway. She's dead now. Last time I saw her, I was a little boy. I don't remember too much about her at all."

We were all quiet for a while. Marshall broke the silence. "I don't know anything about my father . . . or my mother, for that matter."

"You're not the only one. I don't know anything about my parents either," Kieran revealed. "All I know is that I was born in Canada. That's what they tell me, anyway. How I wound up in the United States is beyond me."

This scene revealed one of the major differences between the Cubans and the other kids in the orphanage. Many of the non-Cubans were orphans, and some came from broken families. Although the Pedro Pan children were scattered all over the United States, the vast majority of us would eventually be reunited with our families.

Sadly, a small number never saw their loved ones again.

CHAPTER X

Snow!

We had an early snowfall that autumn. I had never seen snow and imagined it to be something like an immaculately white, woolly cloud. As soon as I got the chance, I excitedly ran outside and jumped into that fluffy substance. Reality soon set in. Much to my chagrin, the snow was cold and wet. Yuck!

That wasn't fun. What to do, then?

Luckily, this was an era free of cell phones and technology. Kids actually had to go outdoors and use their imagination. Inspired by World War Two movies, we could have war games! We searched for long sticks that would serve as rifles, shorter and stubbier sticks for machine guns, and real stubby ones became bazookas. We ran around and hid behind trees, firing at each other.

"You're dead!" we would shout at someone. "You just got killed!"

That one would fall dead, count to ten (real fast), and get up. Now he was another soldier and could go on fighting. To make it more authentic and interesting, we built fortresses and made snowballs, which we called cannonballs.

One of the kids found a book in the rec room that demonstrated how to construct a makeshift catapult. It was very simple by design. All you needed was some rope, elastic bands, and a few tree limbs—and we had plenty of those. We followed the instructions to the letter. I never saw the book, and I can't remember exactly how we did it or why we needed elastic bands, but that catapult was a marvel to behold. It looked more like a gigantic slingshot. It was ingenious!

Except that it didn't work.

We just couldn't get it right. The more we worked at it, the more frustrated we got. If I remember correctly, we placed two tree limbs on the ground next to each other and a third one on top at a ninety-degree angle with the first two. Another limb, placed across, served as a lever. A final one was placed above, perpendicular to the lever.

Of course, I'm going by memory. I'm not sure if any of this is accurate.

Anyway, when that didn't work, we would rearrange the tree limbs in a different order. Finally, it just fell apart.

So, we continued our war games, throwing snow cannonballs at each other—for as long as we could, that is, because eventually we ran out of snow. We would then charge into enemy territory and engage in hand-to-hand combat.

The nuns scrutinized us from afar. One day, two of the older ones came over to us. "You know, boys, you really shouldn't glorify war."

"Oh, Sister," Marshall replied, "it's just make-believe."

"Yeah," Kieran said. "Besides, no one's getting hurt."

The nuns looked at each other and shrugged. The second one sighed and said to the first, resignation in her voice, "Well, as long as they don't kill each other."

Marshall was quick with a quip. "You know how it is with us, Sisters. Boys will be boys!"

When it got dark and very cold, we retreated into the auditorium. There we watched movies the way movies were meant to be watched—on reel-to-reel and projected onto a giant screen. As might be expected, one of my favorites was *The Wizard of Oz*. Every time I saw that scene when Dorothy sang, "Somewhere Over the Rainbow," my heart would melt, and I realized, *Gee, girls are pretty!*

The unspoken rule about girls flashed through my mind again. This time I didn't care and took a chance. I had to tell someone.

"I'm in love with Dorothy!" I confessed to Londri.

"I am so happy for the two of you, Antonio!" Londri said in a smart-alecky way. "But how can that be? Don't you realize that Dorothy is a fictional character? She's not real." Londri just had to spoil my fantasy.

"So?"

"Not only that, but can't you see that Dorothy is, like, fourteen years old, maybe fifteen? Even if she were a real girl, she would be too old for you."

"Well," I thought out loud, "she's not that much older. My mom was one or two years older than my dad."

"Listen, Antonio, Dorothy is played by Judy Garland—an actress. In fact, Judy Garland just happens to be an old lady now! She must be, like, thirty years old!"

That shook me out of my daze. "Thirty years old! Really?" I stared at him, stupefied. "Gee, thanks, Londri, for such good news!"

"Anytime." He smiled at me. "What are friends for?"

"I didn't know Judy Garland was *that* old."

She wasn't ancient. At the time, she was forty years old. But to a ten-year-old, she might as well have been eighty!

◉ ◉ ◉

In the winter we played bingo in the auditorium as well. That was a special treat. The townsfolk donated toys and games so that the kids could win something of value. Sitting at a desk on the stage, one of the nuns would call out a number. Another nun would attach a pin to that number on a giant board. Two or three other nuns would distribute the prizes to the winners. It was exciting and a lot of fun. The nuns seemed to enjoy this activity as much as we did. They made sure that most of us got a prize and enjoyed watching our exhilaration when we received one.

We whiled away many a free afternoon enjoying this exciting, healthy, and wholesome entertainment.

With our winnings, we swapped toys and games. I turned out to be a pretty good negotiator. I amassed a fortune! My treasures included a couple of board games like Parcheesi and Chinese checkers, a blue bowling ball (believe it or not), a toy gun, and a pair of roller skates. I didn't care for the roller skates, so I traded them for a soldier's helmet—

and I don't mean a little toy helmet. I'm talking about a real soldier's helmet!

It sure came in quite handy during our war games.

We wondered where the helmet came from and surmised that one of the townsfolk who had been in the Army probably donated his own helmet. When I left the orphanage, I had to leave the helmet and the rest of my riches behind, but I didn't mind. I knew that they would be fairly distributed among the kids. Besides, it would be rather impractical to travel with them.

☙ ❧

MORE BASKETBALL WOES

Regrettably, the basketball season chugged along on its precarious track. Our next game was against Sacred Heart, another team made up of giants. As customary, Londri and I sat in the bleachers, and I just analyzed the uniforms.

"That's a really nice outfit they're wearing, Londri. I like it a lot."

"Really? Well, I'm not so sure I like it at all," Londri replied. "It's all yellow."

"What's wrong with yellow? It's a nice color—very regal. It reminds me of gold."

"It reminds me of taxi cabs. That's the only thing that's all yellow; that and canaries."

"Get out of here!" I laughed.

We Cuban children had started speaking English with each other, sometimes mixing English and Spanish. The following interaction between Londri and me illustrates this point.

"*¡Mira!* Look at the height of those guys!" Londri murmured.

"*¡Contrá!*" I concurred. "Wow! *¡Son gigantes!* They're giants—terrifically tall!"

"*Terrifically* is not a word, Antonio."

"It's not? Well, it should be."

"Oh yeah?" Londri teased me. "Like you're going to invent a new word in English?"

"Sure! *¡Claro que sí! ¿Por qué no?* Why not?"

"Ha!"

"Okay, Londri, *¿Cómo lo dirías tú?* How would *you* say it?"

"I would just put it like this: they are really tall!"

"Terrifically has a nice sound. In Spanish, I would say *terríficamente*."

"*¿Terríficamente? ¡Ridículo!*" Londri chuckled. "Now *you* get out of here!"

"Anyway," I said, "I think Sacred Heart will probably win this game."

"Really? *¿De veras?* They're gonna slaughter us!"

They did.

The score was forty-five to nine.

◉ ◉ ◉

We continued to receive letters from Mom:

Dear children:

Just a few lines to tell you that there are no jobs for me in Miami, so I decided to move to New York City. That's where I am now. I am living with Lucía and Roberto near the bus terminal on 177th Street until I get settled. This area of New York City is called Washington Heights. Lucía and Roberto are very young and newlyweds. They are only nineteen years old! But one thing about this period in our Cuban diaspora (our exile) is that we all help each other. As for me, my priority is to get a job. That's the main thing. As soon as I do that, I'll get an apartment, and then you can join me.

I just can't wait to hug you both and live together as a family. Pray to God to grant us the grace to grow strong.

I love you both very much.

Mom.

That was the gist of Mom's letter. However, she left out a very important detail. I wrote back quickly, short and straight to the point.

Dear Mom,
We are happy to hear that we may soon be living together. What about Benny?

Her response was not what we wanted to hear:

Dear children
I don't know how to put this in a nice way. It's difficult to get news from Cuba, but the truth is that Benny has not been seen for a while. It is possible that he has been involved in counterrevolutionary activities.
    In the meantime, what we can do is hope and pray.

What Mom left out was that Benny may have been imprisoned.

◉ ◉ ◉

TRAVIS

Travis was an eighteen-year-old alumnus of Saint Vincent's Orphanage. After graduating from Saint Vincent's, he went on to a high school orphanage from which he also graduated. Travis returned to Saint Vincent's as a live-in laborer and handyman doing odd jobs for the nuns. But what he really wanted to be was a barber.

So he gave us haircuts. His favorite was a crew cut, so of course that's the kind of haircut most of the kids wanted. A few of us (like me) didn't like our hair cut that short. And this was 1963, just before the Beatles made their spectacular splash. In a couple of years, long hair would become popular, and no self-respecting boy would even contemplate getting a crew cut.

Travis also loved to take us out on trips. Sometimes he just hung around with us. One thing I'll never forget is the "birthday tradition" he started with the boys. The tradition was to get a spanking from Travis—one spanking for each birthday year.

◉ ◉ ◉

EVEN MORE BASKETBALL WOES

Another basketball game came, and another loss followed.

This time we lost to Saint Thomas. This team was somewhat comparable to Sacred Heart, except that the players on Saint Thomas were not as tall. But they were really good.

"Saint Thomas is wearing a nice, dark-blue color, Londri."

"For once I agree, Antonio," Londri said. "They do have a nice getup."

"I don't think our team stands much of a chance of winning."

"Are you joking? Of course not! Our guys are too little to compete with them!"

"But it's fun watching them try their best."

"As much fun as going to the dentist for a root canal."

I snickered. "What an awful thing to say!"

"It's the truth, Antonio."

I sighed. "Yeah, you're right. It's the truth."

Saint Thomas won handily, forty-one to fourteen.

If you think that was bad, wait until you hear about our second game against Saint John's—a sixty-three to seven shellacking! Saint John's won the championship that year by beating Saint Lawrence, which finished in second place.

Saint Lawrence happened to be the next team we played, our second game against them. Of course, we lost that one, too. The final tally was forty-one to fourteen—the same score as the game against Saint Thomas.

Yes, every team we played had bigger players than we had. But losing was losing. No matter what, it still hurt.

We often sat in the bleachers to watch other teams play after one of our games. I remember watching Saint Francis play Saint Lawrence towards the end of the season. Saint Francis was just a little bit better than we were, and it was the team against whom we had the most success. On the other hand, Saint Lawrence was a powerhouse.

Well, in this particular match, Saint Francis played a very competitive game. The Saint Vincent's kids watching from the bleachers were amazed. With about five minutes to go, Saint Francis trailed Saint Lawrence by only three points, twenty-four to twenty-one. Favian whispered to himself, "Come *on*, Saint Francis!" I thought, *Gee, Favian's actually rooting for Saint Francis to win!* But Saint Lawrence put up a last-minute surge, and Saint Francis lost, thirty-six to twenty-four. Favian looked very disappointed.

Yep, losing was losing.

CHAPTER XI

Thanksgiving

Thanksgiving caught us Cubans by surprise. We were not properly introduced to this traditional holiday, but let me tell you, the meals served at dinner and supper that day were quite a treat! We were served turkey all day. However, only at dinner—the noontime meal—were we regaled with all the trimmings: turkey stuffing, mashed potatoes, gravy, green beans, corn, dinner rolls, cranberry sauce, and, for dessert, apple pie and pumpkin pie.

We still got turkey at supper (in the evening), but the meal itself was lighter.

Dinner began when two cheery nuns appeared in the dining hall. They paraded around the refectory, pushing two utility carts on wheels. Each cart displayed a very large, cooked turkey on a platter.

The children responded excitedly, "Ooh!"

The nuns beamed joyful smiles.

"Wow!" I exclaimed. "Look at the size of those things. I've never seen such gargantuan chickens in my whole life. They are colossal." I informed the boys sitting at my table, "*Gargantuan* and *colossal* are new words I recently learned. They mean real big!"

Kieran broke out laughing. "They are colossal; that's for sure. You can also call them humongous. But I hate to inform you, Antonio, they are not chickens. They are turkeys!"

"Turkeys?"

"Turkeys are big birds," Kieran tried to explain, "much bigger than chickens."

Mateo said the word in Spanish. "*Pavos*. We call them *guanajos* in

Cuba." He turned to Kieran. "You don't see too many turkeys in our country."

"You know," I said, "I have an aunt who ate turkey. She was married to one of my uncles, but I'm not sure what part of Spain her family came from."

"That's funny," Londri commented, "one of my aunts also ate turkey."

"Not in our family," Mateo stated. He asked his brother, "Do you remember ever eating turkey in Cuba?"

"No." Marco shrugged. "Never." Then, turning to the kids at the table, he crossed his eyes and informed them, "You know, guanajo also means silly or dumb."

"*¡El guanajo eres tú!* You are the dumb one!" his brother told him.

The kids laughed.

The cranberry sauce caught my eye. It looked downright suspicious, resembling something like little round balls thrown into a bowl of jelly, and the whole thing was red! I pointed to it and asked my best friend to help me identify it.

"Londri, *¿qué es ésto?* What is this?"

"*¡Yo qué sé, chico!* I've never seen such a thing!"

Chico literally means "small" or "little." It can also signify "young boy." In Cuba it is used as an informal expression which can be translated as "guy" or "man." In this case, Londri's response can be rendered as "I have no idea, man" or "Hey, man, how should I know?"

"Speak English!" Kieran exclaimed.

"What is that?" I inquired, pointing to the red stuff.

"Cranberry sauce," Kieran explained.

"Okay. But what is it?"

"The best way to find out is to try it. Why don't you taste it?"

I took a spoonful and put it on my plate. Then I sampled it.

"Yuck! I don't think I like it," I said. "It's a little sweet, but it's also . . . How do you say the word?" I had been in the orphanage for over six months and spoke English rather well, but I didn't know how to say "bitter," so I said it Spanish: "The taste is *amargo*."

Mateo again came up with the translation. "The word you are looking for is *bitter*."

"Yes, it *is* bitter," Kieran admitted. "But it's also sweet. Basically, it's a fruit."

"A fruit?" I was confused. "But this is not dessert."

Kieran chuckled. "You are right, Antonio. It is not dessert, but it is a fruit."

"You are supposed to eat it along with your turkey," explained Peter, the other Canadian at our table.

"That's very strange," I said.

"In Cuba we never eat fruit and meat together," Londri agreed.

"Well, here we do, and in Canada, too," Kieran stated.

"But in Canada," Peter added, "we don't have cranberry sauce on our Thanksgiving Day."

"Yes, we do!" Kieran corrected him.

"We do?"

"Of course we do!"

Londri asked, "So, you celebrate Thanksgiving in Canada?"

Kieran nodded. "But we celebrate it on the second Monday in October."

"Wait a minute! What did you say?" I was trying to keep up with the conversation. "You said that word before—thanks what?"

"Thanksgiving."

"*Acción de Gracias*," Mateo tried to clarify. "Don't you remember when we had Sister Guadalupe in the summer? She talked about it in class."

"No," I said. "That must have been when I got sick."

"I don't remember Sister Guadalupe talking about it in class," Londri said doubtfully.

"Well, Sister Cordelia mentioned it," Kieran asserted. "Both of you sure looked interested in the story she read about the Pilgrims and the Indians." Today we call them Native Americans.

"Oh yeah, I think I remember now," I admitted.

"Well," Peter butted in, "this is what the Pilgrims and the Indians ate on their first Thanksgiving."

Kieran added, "The Pilgrims, you see, were very grateful to be alive."

Suddenly I remembered the story Sister Cordelia had read to us. She showed us many pictures—illustrations of the Pilgrims first coming to America and struggling through a difficult winter. Peter tried to stimulate our memory.

"Don't you remember the photographs showing how the Indians helped the Pilgrims?"

"Not photographs, you dummy!" Kieran exclaimed. "They didn't have cameras in those days. They were pictures!"

"I know that!" Peter corrected himself. "I meant to say pictures."

Kieran dismissed him with a wave of his hand.

Peter dismissed Kieran in turn. "Sister Cordelia showed us lots and lots of pictures."

Kieran interrupted him. "The pictures showed how the Pilgrims were so grateful to the Indians that they wanted to thank them in a special way."

"So the Pilgrims invited them to a big meal," Peter stated.

"Yes," Londri said, "I remember now."

"But first," I added, "the Pilgrims wanted to thank God."

"That's why it's called Thanksgiving," Peter said, "giving thanks to God."

I turned to Londri and said in a low voice, "Londri, this Thanksgiving of theirs is like our *Noche Buena*."

Londri said thoughtfully, "You know, I suppose you're right."

Noche Buena is not the same as *buenas noches*—which is what you say when you are about to retire for the evening. Noche Buena (literally, the "Good Night") is celebrated on the twenty-fourth of December—that is, on Christmas Eve. All Spanish-speaking countries celebrate Noche Buena by getting the family together for a big banquet.

Each country has its own particular menu. In Cuba, the traditional bill of fare includes *lechón asado* (roast pork), *arroz con frijoles negros* (white rice with black beans), and *yuca* with *mojito*. To a certain extent, yuca is comparable to cassava. Mojito is a sauce consisting of mashed garlic, onions, lemon, and oil. *Maduros* (fried sweet plantains) and *tostones* (fried green plantains) top off the main part of the meal, along with salad, which often consists of *berro* (watercress), lettuce, tomatoes, and onions. Sometimes chunks of avocado are added to the salad.

Flan is the traditional dessert—a type of sweetened egg custard with a caramel topping. *Turrón* (nougat) is also popular. There are many types of turrón. Some are hard and some are soft.

Before Fidel came along, many families would go to church after the Noche Buena feast to attend *la Misa del Gallo,* or Midnight Mass—literally, "the Mass of the Rooster." According to legend, roosters will only crow at midnight on Noche Buena in honor of the birth of the baby Jesus. Friends and families bond during this time of year.

Holidays like Noche Buena and Thanksgiving help create new traditions for future generations. Many countries have similar customs.

☘ ☘ ☘

ABUELO AVELINO

That Thanksgiving night, while lying in bed, my thoughts took me to Abuelo Avelino, my other grandfather. He is the man I baptized when I was born.

How is that possible? Well, let me explain.

My mom was still in the hospital after giving birth to me a few days earlier. The hospital custodians asked her to wait in the hallway while they cleaned the room. So she stepped out, carrying me in her arms. The patient next door was an elderly gentleman. He and my mom struck up a conversation. The man noticed that she looked edgy, pacing back and forth. He asked her if she was all right.

"Gee, I feel awkward telling you this—it's just that—I have to . . ." She was blushing. "All right, I might as well just blurt it out! I have to go to the ladies' room, but I can't take my baby with me, and it seems like the custodians are taking a bit long getting the room settled."

"Oh, don't worry about it," replied the elderly gentleman. "I'll hold the baby while you go to the restroom."

"Oh, no," my mom said, "I wouldn't think of imposing on you."

"You're not imposing. On the contrary, it's no trouble!"

My mom relented. "Well, okay." She did have to go. "You have to take him up in your arms this way and that way, like so—"

"I've had five children of my own and seven grandchildren!" the gentleman replied. "I think I know how to hold a baby."

She looked hesitant. He insisted. "Come on, give him to me. It's no bother at all!"

My mom didn't have much of a choice. She released me and hurried to the ladies' room. She returned soon after, only to discover that I had urinated all over the poor man! She was beside herself.

"I am *so* sorry! Apparently I didn't clip the pin to the diaper as well as I should have. I mean, I have put diapers on babies many times in the past. I'm not a novice at this. How could I be so careless?"

"Don't fret!" the gentleman tried to reassure her. "Listen, this is not the first time I've had a baby pee all over me, and I suspect that it won't be the last!"

"How can you smile? This is not funny!"

"I beg to differ. It *is* funny . . . quite funny if truth be told."

A nurse and an aide happened by and noticed that the gentleman was rather wet. He said to them, "The baby baptized me!" and started to laugh. The nurse and aide giggled as well. My mom must have looked really mortified. The gentleman extended his left hand in greeting and said, "My name is Gilberto Avelino."

She hesitated for a second, looking at his outstretched hand.

"You may be wondering why I'm offering you my left hand instead of my right one. Well, the left one is the dry one."

My mom smiled and they shook hands—left hands, of course. "My name is Noadías, but everyone calls me Nona."

"Nona, your son has claimed me as his own," Mr. Avelino declared. "From now on I will be his new grandfather, Abuelo Avelino. There, you see, I have become his grandfather and, as such, a valued member of your family."

And that's how I acquired a third grandfather.

◉ ◉ ◉

THE NOCHE BUENA PIG

Just like the "Old MacDonald" song goes, Abuelo Avelino had a farm. And on that farm he had some chickens—and ducks and turkeys and geese and all kinds of fowl. He also had cattle and horses and pigs. For the next three years after my birth, while my dad was still living, Abuelo Avelino would present us with a live pig, as a gift, a few weeks before Christmas. My dad's job was to feed the animal in order to get it ready for Noche Buena.

One morning, I was playing Superman in my grandparents' house, wearing a small red blanket on my back as a cape. I was three years old. Suddenly, a man bolted into the house, clutching a squealing, panic-stricken, very large pig by its front legs. The man held the pig's back firmly against his chest because the creature was shaking its legs violently. He had to travel from the front door through the living room, past two bedrooms, the bathroom, the kitchen, the dining room, and the terrace, then climb the stairs to the backyard before he, eventually and very awkwardly, released the pig by dumping it on the ground. And I followed their whole trek through the house, flying like the Superman I was, with my cape gracefully gliding in the air behind me.

The man and the pig were both huffing and puffing from the

exertion. Each seemed relieved that this bizarre episode had come to an end.

The pig was kept in the backyard for the couple of weeks leading to Noche Buena, and my dad made sure that it was well fed. After feeding the pig for those few weeks, my dad butchered it. He did not want the animal to suffer, so he did it quickly. Most people would slay their pigs by cutting their throats. If you didn't know how to do it correctly, the outcome would result in an extremely painful death for the poor creature.

My dad laid the pig down flat on its belly on a table and struck its head forcefully with a baseball bat, killing the animal instantly. He then slit its throat to let all the blood out. I never actually saw him do this. I was told about it.

My dad would have already built a pit in my grandfather's backyard in which to barbecue the pig. The roasting took hours and hours, practically all day, and people took turns rotating the spit.

My dad also built several picnic tables. As best as I can recall, there were two or three rows of tables, with eight to ten chairs per table—more than enough to accommodate the many people who would come. My dad invited family members and the whole neighborhood to partake of the festivities with us. He also made fruit wines. For their part, people would bring food, desserts, and traditional beverages, such as beer, wine, and alcoholic cider. The latter one was a very common Noche Buena drink.

A few years after my dad's death, Abuelo Avelino picked a pony for me as a gift and asked me to name it. I chose to call it Relámpago, which means "Lightning."

Unfortunately, I never got to ride the pony. I never even got the chance to see it. Fidel confiscated Abuelo's farm in the name of the state, and Abuelo had to flee Cuba. He eventually settled in San Antonio, Texas, where many of his relatives lived.

Nonetheless, I can truthfully attest that I once owned a horse.

Abuelo had a very large family, as well as innumerable friends living all over the United States, and he tried to visit as many as he could, including Mom, Norma, and me. He had retired by then and had the time to travel. He dropped in on us a couple times in New Jersey, and spent a few nights with us. He was a devout Baptist and was always quoting biblical passages—a sign of his steadfast belief in the Absolute. Abuelo Avelino was a fine and decent man.

CHAPTER XII

A New Year

Christmas at the orphanage was memorable. We had so many activities that I can't recall them all. But I do remember professional performers treating us to a terrific show in the auditorium—complete with song and dance.

We also put on a Christmas show for the townsfolk, which we performed for a couple of weeks as our way of thanking them for their generosity. They were very involved in the orphanage and were thrilled to see our modest production.

We rehearsed a skit every night for a couple of weeks. One of the girls was chosen to play Mary, the mother of Jesus, and one of the boys was Joseph, her husband. Three kids played the Magi, while two or three kids were angels with wings. The rest of us, including me, were shepherds—except for the few kids who actually played a cow, a donkey, and sheep. We wore corresponding costumes, reenacted the birth of Jesus in a stable, and sang Christmas carols.

The townsfolk got a kick watching us entertain them, especially when we forgot our lines or got them mixed up. They were so supportive of us that several families took a few of the kids into their own homes for a weekend. Once they got to know each other, some families opened their doors to these children for occasional visits. A few households even petitioned the courts to become the youngsters' legal guardians.

After each recital, we would invite the townsfolk to join us for refreshments. During one of these, Sister Cordelia introduced Norma and me to a woman who had the same last name as ours.

"My maiden name is also Dora," she informed us, smiling, "just like yours."

"Really?" I was surprised. "Gee, I thought our family was the only one with that last name! Is your family from Cuba or from Spain?" I asked the lady.

"Actually, we are Slavic."

"Eslavic?" Norma and I looked at each other curiously. Neither of us had heard of the word.

The lady corrected our mispronunciation. "The appropriate way to say it is Slavic."

"Slavic," Norma and I repeated at the same time.

"That's right!" the lady declared. "My family came from Russia and Czechoslovakia."

Norma seemed shocked. "No!" she exclaimed.

"But those are Communist countries!" I interjected.

"Nowadays they are," she said with a grin, "but let me assure you, *we are not Communists!*"

We spoke with the lady about Russia and Czechoslovakia for a while. She gave us a brief history lesson and a perspective of the political situation. She also told us about her family and how they came to the United States.

Alas, we never heard from the woman again.

☉ ☉ ☉

THE CHEMISTRY SET

A few days later, while the D6 boys were playing cards and board games in the rec room, I came across a magazine with an advertisement for a chemistry set. The set came in a folding metal box, beautifully illustrated, which opened into four compartments. The contents inside revealed a myriad of colorful liquid chemicals in small jars, along with vials, test tubes, and supplies. I was intrigued and showed it to Londri.

"Look at this, Londri! It reads, *Join the ranks of amateur scientists.*"

"Let me see." Londri took the magazine. "It says, *Atomic energy*."

Marshall, who was within earshot, grabbed the magazine from Londri to get a closer view and exclaimed, "Atomic energy? Wow!"

"I'd love to have one of these," I whispered.

"I don't know." Londri was cautious. "Atomic energy sounds dangerous."

"If it's in a magazine," Marshall contended, "it's because it's safe."

"Yeah," I agreed. "A magazine wouldn't publish something that's dangerous!"

"I'm with you." Favian had been listening to the conversation and placed his hand on Londri's shoulder. "You don't want to mess with atomic energy." He leaned over Marshall's back to peek at the magazine ad.

"I'm telling you guys," Marshall argued, "if it's written in a magazine, then it's gotta be safe."

"Look at the cost!" Favian pointed to the price. "It's really expensive."

I can't recall how much it was, but I had to agree with Favian. "Yes, I can see that," I said forlornly. "Still, I'd love to get my hands on one of those."

That night I tossed and turned in bed, thinking about this dilemma. Suddenly, I arrived at the solution: *los Reyes Magos*—the Three Wise Kings. The Magi!

Why didn't I think of them before? They would most definitely bring me the chemistry set if I asked them for it. I decided to dispatch them a letter in the morning.

And just in case the Reyes Magos didn't deliver, guess who else I could write to?

Santa!

◉ ◉ ◉

CHRISTMAS

The townsfolk couldn't have been more generous to us. They donated toys and games to be distributed among us as Christmas gifts. They had gifts for girls, gifts for boys, and gifts for both genders, such as books and board games.

Moreover, we were regaled with a wonderful concert in which numerous musicians came to sing for us. I was particularly impressed with an African American woman who called herself Aunt Jemima and dressed as the character on the pancake box. This was December 1962, after all, and no one gave the political correctness—or rather, incorrectness—much thought, including herself, obviously. She sang "He's Got the Whole World in His Hands" and got us to sing along with her and to gesture with our hands.

"When you sing the line 'He's got the whole world,' cup your hands as if you are holding something round," she said. "This is symbolic of our planet Earth. And when you sing the line 'in his hands,' extend your hands outward." She showed us by displaying the palms of her hands. "This is symbolic of the palm of God's hands."

She continued, "The next verse goes 'He's got the itty-bitty baby in his hands,' but we are going to change it to 'He's got the itty-bitty children in his hands.' When we sing that verse, you point to your chests with both of your thumbs. After all, when you get right down to it, *you all* are God's itty-bitty children."

As we sang that verse, she extended her arms out from left to right, panning us, and, as she had directed, we pointed to our chests with our thumbs.

When she bade us farewell, we applauded her enthusiastically. Some of the children had tears in their eyes. She had truly touched our hearts. Even the usually forgetful Norma remembers this performance.

One of the other entertainers got us to sing Christmas carols and other familiar songs, like "Old McDonald Had a Farm." Then the last act was reserved for a very unique and much beloved person. We got a hunch as to who this particular guest was when we sang "Santa Claus Is Coming to Town." And when we heard the familiar "Ho ho ho! Meeerry Christmas, everybody! Ho ho ho!" we knew that we were in for a special treat.

The smallest children broke into a chorus of "Santa! Santa!" However, this enthusiasm wasn't reserved for the little ones. In fact, many of us, including myself, believed in Santa Claus.

Yes, at the age of ten, I still believed in Santa Claus, okay? Of course, I knew that the Santa Claus we saw on stage was just an actor. I was also totally aware that the real Santa Claus was quite busy with his elves and reindeer up in the North Pole, getting ready to distribute toys on Christmas Eve.

Santa's helpers carried a huge throne onto the stage, and he sat on it. The little ones were brought to him, and they sat on his lap. Santa would ask, "And what would you like for Christmas, little girl?" or "What would you like for Christmas, little boy?"

We all enjoyed it when the tots voiced their wishes, especially when a little boy tried to pull Santa's whiskers off and articulated his wish for Christmas: "I want a horshey, Santa—a lil' horshey pony!"

Everyone laughed and clapped. We all got a kick out of this, especially the townsfolk.

The following day, we visited the other sports ground—the one that had a big baseball field with bleachers. I have no idea why, but I was sitting on the grass with one of the boys from D6. He said to me, "The big kids keep saying that there is no Santa Claus, but I believe in Santa Claus! How about you?"

I didn't realize that he was setting me up. "Ah, yes. I sure do!"

"Ha ha ha!" He ridiculed me. "You wimp! You're such a sissy!" He turned to some of the bigger boys walking nearby and proclaimed, "Hey, fellas, this big wuss still believes in Santa Claus! Can you believe it?"

To add salt to injury, the big kids burst out laughing, too.

A few days later, my mom phoned to wish us a merry Christmas and a happy *Reyes Magos*. Celebrated on January 6, the Epiphany, when the Three Wise Kings presented the baby Jesus with gifts of gold, frankincense, and myrrh, Reyes Magos is when kids in Spanish-speaking countries receive their Christmas gifts.

"Mom, tell me the truth: is there such a thing as Santa Claus? Is he real? How about los Reyes Magos?"

"No, Tony, there is no Santa Claus. The Reyes Magos gave the child Jesus gifts, but not to the children of today."

"Why didn't you tell me the truth, Mom? The kids here are making fun of me!"

"Tony, children need fantasy, magic, and fairy tales. That's the reason why we tell them these enchanting stories. Parents from every country do this. It's a beautiful tradition."

"Well, I'm not a child anymore, Mom!"

"That's right, Tony. You are ten years old. You're growing up. I'm very sorry I didn't tell you sooner."

I realized that my mom felt a little guilty and decided this was the opportune time to ask for a particular gift. I suddenly blurted out, "I want a chemistry set for Christmas! I wrote Santa Claus and los Reyes Magos asking for one. I didn't know what address to write on the envelopes, but Sister Cordelia said she would mail the letters. But as it turns out, Mom, *you* are Santa Claus and los Reyes Magos all rolled up into one."

"Well, Tony . . ." She was silent for a while. "We'll see."

Later I felt guilty for requesting such an expensive gift. We certainly were not rich, and the Communist regime had confiscated the few possessions we had in Cuba. Besides, Mom had just arrived in the United States and was looking for work. It was very self-centered of me to make such a request.

I prepared a quick letter following my greedy appeal:

Dear Mom:
It was real good talking to you on the telephone. One thing we didn't talk about is that they are real nice people here at the orphanage,

and they are taking real good care of us. You were right about that. By the way, Mom, don't send me the chemistry set I asked for. On second thought, it was very selfish of me to make such a stupid request. I am very sorry that I ever even mentioned it.

Too late. The chemistry set arrived a few days after I sent the letter. As advertised, the set came in a huge metal box. And like the announcement in the magazine affirmed, it contained quite an assortment of colorful liquid chemicals in small jars, along with vials, test tubes, metal wires, and other supplies. In addition, it came with a magnifying glass, thermometer, and instruction manual.

The set attracted a lot of attention. I was very generous with it, and some of the kids experimented with the chemicals. I tried making peace with Wyatt and asked him if he wanted to help me with it. I handed him the instructions. "Maybe you can help me figure this out."

"Nah," he replied. "I never read instructions. They're boring!"

This was probably the closest and friendliest contact I ever had with Wyatt. Favian came around to act as a buffer. And, of course, Marshall and Londri were there to lend a hand as well.

Wyatt was right. We all found the instructions too complicated and boring. It was easier just to fool around with the various chemicals and mix them haphazardly. We would fiddle with the set for thirty minutes or so, make a mess, and give up. We would go back to it the next day and repeat the process, but in the end, we always got bored.

The ad in the magazine had hyped this product as atomic energy. We certainly never got close to atomic energy. All we ever got by mixing chemicals together was a bit of faint smoke and a foul smell—like rotten eggs.

Atomic energy, my foot!

Eventually, I took the box set to the ground floor in the back by the parking lot, where we used to eat watermelon during the summer. The nuns would arrange a spread of the fruit on long picnic tables outside.

We could pick a slice of any size and eat as much of it as we wanted. I wondered if the watermelon came from the farmer who had complained to Mother Superior that her boys were illegally helping themselves to his bounty.

On the subject of the chemistry set, the ground floor in the back by the parking lot was perfect for me. At this point, nobody wanted to play with it anyway. I would just roam around indoors near the laundry room and kitchen. There, I could play with the chemistry set by myself in total peace and quiet. But I soon got tired of the whole thing.

Ah, but the guilt engulfed me. I kept thinking about how costly and difficult it must have been for my mother to send me such an expensive gift. And I had gotten sick of it! I had been so egocentric and narcissistic.

Notwithstanding, there was an unintended and pleasantly surprising outcome to wandering off on the ground floor.

Somebody in the vicinity must have had a radio, because I remember hearing the songs "Sherry" and "Big Girls Don't Cry" by the Four Seasons, as well as "Surfin' Safari" by the Beach Boys. These songs were very popular in those days. I liked this kind of music. It was fun and it had a happy beat.

A very satisfying realization came to me: I had a pretty good understanding of the lyrics. I was becoming fluent in English!

◉ ◉ ◉

A NEW WARDROBE

A few days after the holidays, Sister Cordelia came to me with a strange announcement: "Antonio, we want you to be fitted for new pants and shirts."

The announcement wasn't that strange at all; in fact, it was long overdue. For the longest time, I had been wearing pants that were way too big for me. All that exercise on the playground and a healthy diet helped me lose weight. To keep my pants from sliding off me, I kept piercing holes on my belt with the prong in the buckle to tighten the pants around my waist.

It never occurred to me to ask for new clothes. We kids didn't think of complaining about such things. We accepted our reality—that is, the way things were in the orphanage. The nuns stretched the clothes we wore for as long as they could, including shoes and supplies. They had to. I think we all appreciated that the orphanage was not a wealthy organization. We depended on charity, and the townsfolk always responded generously.

Hence, it never occurred to me to ask for nail clippers or small scissors in order to clip my nails. I just cut my fingernails and toenails with my own fingernails. It took a little practice, but I became quite adept at it. Soap and toothpaste were distributed on a regular basis, but when it came to minor supplies, such as shampoo, we just washed our hair with hand soap. We didn't give it much thought. Some kids wore sneakers that were so ragged and ripped that they were practically falling off their feet. But they didn't complain. They wore them proudly.

So I was quite intrigued by Sister Cordelia's announcement that I was going to get new clothes.

"Follow me, Antonio."

She led me to a room on the first floor I had never seen before. About four or five ladies sat at tables, crocheting. A couple of them sat behind sewing machines. I put on a pair of new navy-blue pants and stood on a small platform while another lady took my measurements with a ribbon of cloth. I was also given a new white shirt to try on. A full-length mirror was positioned in front of the platform. I glanced at the reflection and was stunned at what I saw—a tall and fine-looking ten-year old boy. His blond hair was parted on the left, and his bangs were combed up in a pompadour. And that boy was skinny.

I liked the way he looked—the way *I* looked. I caught myself smiling. The ladies smiled too. They glanced at me approvingly as they crocheted.

They also took my height and weight—four feet seven inches and ninety-nine pounds. When I first entered the orphanage, I was four feet three and weighed one hundred nineteen pounds after gaining weight at the Florida City camp. This was great! I had gotten taller and lost weight. And now I had brand-new garments that matched my new figure.

I displayed my new attire for the first time when we assembled for supper. The guys were amazed and impressed. Melody was impressed, too. As luck would have it, she and I entered the refectory at the same time. She bumped against me, on purpose, shoved me flirtatiously, and giggled. Our eyes met and she smiled that adoring smile of hers. I smiled as well.

Wait a minute! I rebuked myself. *What's the matter with me?*

Naturally, I swiftly looked away. And from the corner of my eye, I caught Norma's sly grin. As usual, Kieran noticed Melody's admiring eyes. Favian and Marshall just shrugged. Londri took his cue from them and smiled weakly.

Kieran followed his observation with his typical refrain: "Antonio has a girlfriend!"

I opened my mouth to respond but decided not to. *What's the point? I've had enough of this ridiculous rule that boys are not supposed to like girls!* By their reactions, Favian, Marshall, and Londri had apparently had enough of it also.

We were all growing up.

I just shook my head and decided to say, "Let's eat!"

After the nuns led us in prayer and we took our seats, Londri studied me, his mouth wide open in surprise. "You look great, Antonio!"

"We knew you had lost some weight," Peter said, "but we couldn't tell how skinny you'd gotten because of those baggy pants you wore!"

The other guys at the table slapped me on the back in congratulations.

Yep, it felt good. Real good.

Unfortunately, however, in all of my time at the orphanage, Melody and I never spoke one word to each other.

◉ ◉ ◉

A TRANSFORMATION

The kids were not the only ones who complimented me on my new look. Sister Cordelia was also pleased.

"We want you to look your very best," she said, "so that when you and your sister get together with your mom and dad, they will be able to appreciate that we took good care of you."

"It's only my mother, Sister. My father died when I was four years old. He had cancer. Leukemia."

"Ah, yes, I believe I read about it when I saw your file. I'm so sorry to hear that, Antonio."

"What happens when we die, Sister?" I asked abruptly.

She was taken aback by my question. "I think that you know the answer." She paused and observed me skeptically before replying. "We go to heaven."

"Yeah, but some people go to hell. Right?"

"Hell is for evil people, Antonio. That's where really bad people go." She looked at me tentatively. "Why are you asking me about this?"

"My father was a good man, Sister. Do you think he is in heaven?"

"Of course, Antonio! The Church teaches us that all good people go to heaven."

"Yes, I know that, but . . . where is heaven? What does heaven look like, exactly?"

"It serves us no purpose to waste our time thinking such thoughts, Antonio. Don't think of heaven simply as a place."

"Heaven is not a place?"

"Heaven is a mystery. It's where we will all be in union with God."

"But how? I mean, my question really is what happens, in reality, in actual fact, when we die? Where do we actually go?"

"Let me put it this way: when we die, we will be transformed."

"Transformed?"

"Again, it really is useless to think such thoughts. The transformation I am talking about is a mystery."

"Like God is a mystery?"

"No one truly understands this mystery, Antonio, but let me assure you, it'll be wonderful. It will be a transformation beyond our imaginings and expectations, further than where our thoughts and dreams could ever possibly take us. We will be transformed, and it will be wonderful."

I raised my eyebrows in astonishment and scratched my forehead. The fact that Sister Cordelia was so sure that it would be wonderful gave me a certain sense of peace. I wasn't so sure I understood the whole picture Sister Cordelia had painted, but I was content to know that I wasn't the only one who did not completely comprehend it.

From that day on, I held Sister Cordelia in much higher regard than in the past. Sister Kevin she was not, but of course not! She could not possibly be anything like Sister Kevin.

She was Sister Cordelia.

◉ ◉ ◉

ANOTHER LETTER

Soon after this conversation with Sister Cordelia, Norma and I received another letter from our mom:

Dear children,
I have good news. I got a job working in a factory, sewing. It's minimum wage, but it's a paycheck. For now this is the way it has to be. I am still living with Lucía and Roberto, and they couldn't be any nicer, but it's not fair to such a young and newlywed couple like them. I have to find a better place in which to live.
Here's the bad news. This town just isn't suitable for us. It's not suitable for Lucía and Roberto, either. They know that. Living near the bus terminal on 177th Street in Washington Heights is not a good place in which to bring up children. They want to have children of their own, and I have the two of you. So I have to look for

a better area. Rest assured that I am quite resolute in my quest. I am certain that I will find a nice place for us. In the meantime, we have to hope and trust that the Lord is with us, that God will always lead us and will always keep us safe.
Remember this. Believe it.

With love always,
Mom

That night, as I lay in bed, I had another memory of my father. I guess my mom's letter prompted it. My dad had just gotten home from work and went to kiss Mom, who was busy in the kitchen. He said he was exhausted. Norma and I were in bed, lying on our backs. For some reason, we had our shoes on. I raised my feet and playfully called out, "¡Los zapatos, los zapatos!" (The shoes, the shoes!)

Of course, I was trying to get Daddy's attention so that he would take our shoes off. Norma imitated me. She raised her feet, and we both called out, "¡Los zapatos, los zapatos!"

Dad smiled and came over to the bed. "Ah, so you want me to take your shoes off, eh?"

"Yeah!" we both replied.

"Oh," he said, "but I'm so tired. I've been working all day!"

"Aw," Norma moaned.

"Come on, Daddy!" I was more insistent. "Take our shoes off!"

"Yeah!"

Dad started laughing. Mom came over, chuckling as well.

"Okay, children," Dad said, "we'll take your shoes off."

Dad made believe that he was going to unfasten my shoelaces. Instead, he said, "What's wrong with your pajamas?"

He started to unbutton my pajama shirt, swiftly flung it open, then sank his face on my belly and made a flatulent sound, causing his cheeks to puff up. It gave me the shivers but also made me snicker. Mom started tickling my sister. Norma and I were twisting and turning and giggling.

Then he started tickling my belly.

"Stop, Daddy, stop!" I implored him.

"Oh, no," Dad said, "you asked for it; now you're gonna get it!"

He kept blowing on my tummy. Mom did the same to Norma. The four of us couldn't control our laughter.

That is a fond memory.

◉ ◉ ◉

THESE NEVER-ENDING BASKETBALL WOES!

Meanwhile, the basketball season was drawing to a close. We played two more games against Saint Joseph's. The score against the younger kids was not a blowout, for once: twenty-one to fourteen. I played in that game, but I wasn't on the court very long, maybe a minute or so. I'm not sure why Father stuck me in there. I couldn't play to save my life! When I first started playing the sport, I stank to the high heavens. Two weeks after that, I was terrible. A week later, I was pretty bad. Now I was just bad.

That sounds like an improvement, right? In my defense, I have to repeat that I never played basketball in Cuba. All in all, I only played in two games during the whole season for a total of two minutes, and never in a million years did I come close to scoring a basket. I did get to hold the ball once, dribbling it for a couple seconds before the other team stole it from me.

True to form, our oldest players also lost that day—this time, by a score of twenty-eight to fifteen.

However, our twelfth and final game was against Saint Francis, and it was glorious, if defeat can be called glorious. It gave us hope. With just a minute or two to go, we actually found ourselves leading by twenty to eighteen! We couldn't believe it! Favian was a wizard on the court, moving with speed and agility. You should have seen him.

Much to our dismay, Saint Francis rallied to tie the score with just a few seconds to go and went on to score another basket at the buzzer, winning by twenty-two to twenty. Notwithstanding, we took pride in our hero. Favian shone in defeat. He was a dynamo on the court and full of energy—a sight to behold!

CHAPTER XIII

Eleven

MARCH 30, 1963

The birthday tradition Travis initiated was quite a ritual. We would get one spanking for each birthday year. For example, if it was your tenth birthday, you got spanked ten times; eleventh birthday, eleven spankings; and so on. These were real thrashings, mind you. There was nothing delicate about them.

And this is the weirdest thing about being a boy: we actually looked forward to getting a big, bad spanking from Travis. I was like the others. I couldn't wait for my birthday.

On the day I turned eleven, Travis told me, "You're gonna get it, kiddo! You just don't know exactly when and you don't know exactly where. But don't you worry none, my dear boy, you *are* gonna get it! It's gotta be at the right time, and it's gotta be in the right place."

The expectation was agonizing.

We were in a park near the orphanage. We must have had a picnic or a barbecue that day, because we were inside a picnic shelter filled with picnic tables. I don't remember the precise location or how we got there, but the excitement was palpable. All the kids knew that it was my turn, and Travis took his sweet time. He was the master of suspense. He would glance at me, open his mouth for a few seconds as if he were about to speak, then close his mouth and look away.

He led us inside that building, and we came to a stop in front of his chosen picnic table. He pointed to that table and motioned with his head for me to lie on it, flat on my stomach.

Londri helped me up. Looking at me with a grave expression, he stated solemnly, with concern in his voice, "I'm here with you, buddy. All the way." Then he added, smirking, "This is gonna hurt you more than it is gonna hurt me."

Marshall said, "That goes double for me!"

"And triple for me," added Favian.

Marshall held his rear end and yelped, "I'm in pain! Oh, it hurts real bad!"

"Get outta here!" I snapped at them, grinning. "Wise guys."

All the kids gathered round the sacrificial table, their eyes the color of blood, licking their lips, salivating in anticipation of my imminent butchering.

Travis slowly lifted his right arm as if he were going to whack me. He kept his arm suspended in the air, turned to the other kids, and asked gently, in a muted whisper, "Whatta ya think, boys—soft or hard?"

Of course, all the boys shouted, "Hard! Hard! Hard!"

Travis then addressed me: "You heard the verdict, Antonio. Your own brothers have declared that they want you to . . . suffer."

The kids continued the chorus: "Hard! Hard! Hard!"

I closed my eyes and braced myself for my fate. Travis unleashed ten merciless spankings. They were fierce. Brutal.

Naturally, the kids counted the spankings. "One! Two! Three!"

After the tenth one, Travis stopped. "Wait a minute." He asked the kids in that gentle, muted voice of his, "Is he ten or eleven years old? I can't remember."

The children yelled back, "Eleven! Eleven! Eleven!"

"Oh," replied Travis, slowly, deliberately. "So, that means he gets one more?"

"One more! One more! One more!"

"Soft . . . or hard?"

The children repeated their refrain. "Hard! Hard! Hard!"

Travis's arm went up again and came down fast but stopped abruptly, just a few inches from its target. His arm seemed to hesitate in the air for an instant. Then Travis patted me gently on the backside.

The children expressed their disappointment. "Awww!"

"What's the matter, guys?" Travis teased them. "Wasn't that last one hard enough? You mean to tell me y'all want a real hard one?"

"Hard! Hard! Hard!"

"But I already gave him eleven! What else can I do?"

"Come on, whatcha waitin' for?" Wyatt shoved Travis against the table. "Smack 'im real hard this time and make 'im cry like a *girrrl!*"

"One more?" Travis was really enjoying this. "But that would make it twelve . . . and he's eleven."

"For crying out loud, whack 'im already!" Wyatt shouted. "Let 'im have it real hard! Just do it!"

One way or another, in his mind, Wyatt had to get even with me.

The rest of the kids roared, "Do it! Do it! Do it!"

"You heard your brothers," Travis told me. "Well, this last one's number twelve. Guess it's gotta count for next year."

And he launched the hardest, nastiest, most painful one yet. It was so hard that the table shook. Up and down it went, and me with it, as if we had been struck and blown away by an explosion.

The children howled and clapped. I lay flat on the table, tongue hanging out, in agony and out of breath.

After a few seconds, Londri, Favian, and Marshall helped me off the picnic table and onto my feet. I felt sore and was gasping for breath, my legs wobbly.

Travis asked me, in an innocent, singsong voice, "How do you feel, Antonio?"

"Fine!" I replied. "Never felt better. Didn't hurt a bit!"

"Yeah, right!" Wyatt intoned, eyes wild with delight.

The funny thing is, I felt proud. I had undertaken a rite of passage and passed with flying colors. I had been initiated into adulthood. I was a man.

Exactly one month later, regrettably, I was gone. My turn had come to depart the orphanage.

THE RIGHT PLACE AT THE RIGHT TIME

As far as I can recollect, life at the orphanage revolved around the playground. I don't remember much about classroom instructions, but I do remember watching television. The small screen was an excellent vehicle in promoting English fluency. There were a lot of great programs at the time. My favorites were *Leave It to Beaver*, *My Three Sons*, *The Patty Duke Show*, and *Make Room for Daddy* because they revolved around family life, which I really missed; but as I reflect on my time at the orphanage during my final days there, I can say that the prevailing sense was one of contentment. I would have said, "This is exactly where I belong." If I could now summon the boy I was in 1963—if I could not only get into his skin but *become* that boy again—I would confirm that I had an awareness and appreciation for being in the right place at the right time, even at that tender age.

Of course, I am not sure that I could have expressed this in such a manner at the time. Years had to go by—decades had to fly by!—for this realization to take root. Saint Vincent's Orphanage was a community: *my* community. It felt right. I experienced a sense of tranquility. I integrated into that place. I felt a kind of respect for it, and in turn, I felt that I was respected as a valued member of that community.

It also helped that many of the kids looked up to me. I can't assert that they all did. Wyatt was definitely one of the exceptions. But I think that he changed. At least, that's what I want to believe. Perhaps Favian and Marshall became a good influence on Wyatt, though the fight in the showers may have had something to do with it. Whatever the case, in the end, Wyatt stopped bullying me.

For the most part, I felt myself to be complete and whole. It's funny how such a feeling can be experienced by a young child. It's a privilege that some people never experience.

I was blessed.

I was a Pedro Pan kid, for crying out loud!

◉ ◉ ◉

THE EASTER EGG HUNT
APRIL 14, 1963

We didn't have Easter egg hunts in Cuba. This was a completely new tradition for me. I was intrigued by these colored, hard-boiled eggs dispersed all over the church grounds. Ah, but most of the eggs were hidden; you had to look for them!

The townsfolk gleefully handed out small wicker baskets to the children as we entered church wearing our Sunday best. Mass wouldn't start for another thirty minutes.

A very tall and skinny man with a goatee addressed me. "Howdy there, young feller, welcome to our Easter egg hunt! Here y'are," he said, giving me a basket. "Now go fetch as many of them there eggs as ye kin fine an' chuck'em in there, in that there basket." He glanced over the surroundings and said, "There's lotsa kids clear out over there already! I reckon ya best mosey on down yonder lickety split if ya wanna git any eggs. Yep. I reckon so, I reckon."

I knew that he wanted me to fill the basket with eggs, but his terminology was unfamiliar to me, although it did seem to share some elements with the English language. Was he speaking a tongue similar to English, the way Italian and Portuguese are similar to Spanish? I walked a few feet away from him, out of earshot, and approached Marshall. Favian was close by.

"Hey, Marshall," I asked him, whispering, "what did that man say we're supposed to do with these baskets?"

Marshall whispered back, "He said you gotta hunt for eggs and put them in the baskets."

"Hunt? For eggs?"

"That's right."

He noticed my confused look. "Well, my dear Antonio"—he spoke in that special tone that only he possessed—"why on earth do you suppose they call it an Easter egg *hunt*?"

"¡Qué sé yo!" I used the Spanish expression I had taught them, and then said it in English. "How should I know? What does it mean?"

"It means," Favian chimed in, "that you have to hunt for eggs."

"I don't get it. Please tell me again. Why do we have to hunt for eggs?"

"Because it's Easter!" Marshall retorted loudly. "You know, I wish you hadn't learned English so good. You're always asking too many questions."

I was motivated by a desire to speak English fluently. I didn't realize that perhaps my many questions were not always appreciated. To add fuel to the fire, I had started correcting the native speakers of English whenever they made grammatical mistakes.

"Don't say that I learned English so *good*, Marshall. The proper form is to say so *well*." Then I hammed it up. "Or so *correctly*, or so *fluently*."

Marshall shook his head and looked at Favian for support. "See what I mean?"

"I love it!" Favian laughed. "Keep it up, Antonio. You're doing great! Before you know it, you're gonna be *learning* us real proper English."

"You're not helping, Favian!" Marshall protested.

"Listen, guys," I said, "I don't mean to make a big thing out of this, but I just don't get this hunting thing. If we're supposed to be hunting, shouldn't we be hunting animals for food and using bows and arrows or rifles?"

"Yes, you're right, you *are* making a big thing out of this," Marshall replied. Then he shouted in exasperation, "It's not that kind of hunt!"

"I see." I shook my head and smiled. "You really don't know the reason, do you?"

"It's called a *hunt*!" All of a sudden, Marshall didn't seem to be in a good mood.

"It's called a *hunt*, but that's just an expression," Favian chimed in to explain. "It's an Easter egg hunt because it's Easter Sunday."

"Oh, right, yeah. It's Easter Sunday. That explains everything."

Marshall shouted, "It's a tradition!"

"All right already. You don't have to get so excited, and you don't have to yell at me."

"I'm not yelling!" Marshall yelled. He lowered his voice. "I'm very calm." He extended his hand to show it was steady. "See?"

"Now," Favian said, "what you gotta do, right now, is go hunt!"

I realized that neither Marshall nor Favian could explain the tradition. The truth is, they knew nothing about it.

Later that day, I was introduced to another strange tradition: the Easter chocolate bunny. It sort of went hand in hand with the tradition of the Easter eggs. And for all the tea in China, I could make absolutely no sense of this tradition either. But I certainly enjoyed eating it!

◉ ◉ ◉

THE ANNOUNCEMENT

A week or so later, Sister Cordelia approached me as we were departing the refectory after supper. "We have good news for you and your sister."

I took a guess at what she was going to say. "My mother is coming."

"*She* is not coming. *You* are going." She placed her hand on my shoulder. "You are going home, Antonio!"

"We're going back to Cuba?" I was shocked. "You mean, Fidel Castro got kicked out?"

"No, no, no. Would that we could be so lucky!" Sister Cordelia clarified the news. "You're going to New Jersey. Your mom has claimed the both of you. You must be very happy!"

Honestly, I wasn't. I did not want to leave the orphanage. I loved it there! I wanted my mother to come and live in Indiana.

I gasped for air. "New Jersey, eh?" I was silent for a few seconds. All I could think to ask was "When are we leaving?"

"Tomorrow morning. Early."

This came as a shock. I wasn't expecting to hear such news this soon—but, of course, it really wasn't that soon. The date was April 29, 1963. We had been at Saint Vincent's Orphanage since May 3, 1962, just three days short of a full year. It didn't strike me at the time that April 29 was the anniversary of my father's death. He had been dead for seven years.

Sister Cordelia added, "I know that you were recently fitted with new clothes, but we want you to go home with another pair of new pants."

"A new pair?" My mouth dropped open in surprise.

Sister Cordelia smiled and said, "Come on, follow me."

She led me back to the fitting room on the first floor. The same four or five ladies sat crocheting at their tables. They smiled when they saw me.

Another lady motioned to me to stand on the scale. She weighed me and took my height, then had me stand on the small platform and took my measurements with a ribbon of cloth as she had the last time. I glimpsed my image in the full-length mirror and was pleased with my reflection.

I waved at the eleven-year-old boy, and he waved right back at me.

"Is it my imagination, or am I taller and thinner than before?"

"It's your imagination," she informed me. She took a closer look at the scale. "Yes, you grew not quite a quarter of an inch, more or less. You're now four feet seven and a quarter inches tall. And your weight is the same: ninety-nine pounds."

"We are going to miss you!" said one of the ladies.

"But we're also very happy for you!" another one added.

"Thank you," I answered, nodding. A little emotional, I stared down at my feet. I didn't want them to see my misty eyes.

PART FOUR

Impermanence

*Buddha taught
that the only constant
is change.*

CHAPTER XIV

Nothing Lasts Forever

"All things must pass," as George Harrison sang after the breakup of the Beatles. Whether he realized it or not, his thoughts were rather Buddhist in nature.

Nothing lasts forever. Everything changes.

That's life!

On the one hand, I truly missed my mom and was happy at the prospect of reconnecting with her and living as a family. On the other hand, I felt a profound sadness knowing that I had to leave Saint Vincent's Orphanage, this magnificent and absolutely wonderful place that had become my home, never to see it again! And what was worse, never again to see any of my D6 buddies, friends who had become brothers. We were family!

This was another sorrowful goodbye in my young life.

◉ ◉ ◉

SEPARATION

I returned to my dormitory to hang up my new pair of pants in my locker. Sister Cordelia was waiting for me. "Don't mind the locker, Antonio." She pointed to a small suitcase lying on the floor beside my bed. "You have to pack, child. You will be leaving very early in the morning, before any of the others wake up."

"Yes, I understand." I turned to look at her. I thought this was a perfect opportunity to express my gratitude. "Thank you, Sister. Thank you for all you've done for me."

"You are more than welcome, Antonio." She raised her arms and waved them in a circular motion around the dormitory. "This is my vocation, my mission. All the children—that includes you, Antonio—are my mission."

I nodded and gazed down at the suitcase for quite some time, as if in a trance, wondering whether to pack now or later.

Sister Cordelia spoke softly. Her voice was gentle. "If you desire, Antonio, I will be more than happy to help you pack."

With moist eyes, I glanced at her. "I do appreciate your kindness, Sister." I was trying very hard to keep from crying. "But my mother taught Norma and me . . . how to . . ."—in spite of my effort, my voice revealed my grief—"how to fold our clothes and pack." I inhaled deeply, held my breath for an instant, and exhaled slowly. "I can do this." My thoughts trailed off momentarily. "It's just that . . ."

There was a long pause.

"It's just that what, Antonio?"

"May I go outside, Sister?" I replied abruptly. "I think that I would like to take one last look around the playground. I don't want to forget what it looks like. I won't be long."

"Of course, my child. Take your time."

"But first"—I gestured with my hand to indicate the dormitory—"I would like to look over this place. If I may."

"Absolutely, Antonio! Suit yourself."

Sorry to say, I didn't have a camera. As far as I know, there are no photographs of Norma or me at Florida City or Saint Vincent's Orphanage. I never saw anyone take our picture.

I walked the length of the dormitory, starting from my bed. I ambled along the windows on the right side, on to the rear of our sleeping quarters and down the other side. From time to time I would stop to examine the rows of beds. Occasionally, I came to a halt and slid my hand along one of the bedposts.

I glanced at the lockers before me, made my way there, and bowed, demonstrating my respect for them. Then I turned towards the lavatory. I went to my sink where I had the altercation with Wyatt—the place where he had picked me up and violently dragged me all the way against the wall. I went to the wall and placed my hand on it.

From there I strolled past the toilets and to the showers in the rear. I paused and inspected them for a few seconds. I made an about-face and proceeded to the stairs and the first floor.

Upon reaching ground level, I stepped outside and took in the panorama. I slowly meandered in the direction of the playground, stopping periodically to observe the terrain—the building where we lived and, before it, the water tower, the basketball court, the baseball field, the picnic tables, the swings.

Ah, the swings! The memory of my brawl with Mateo flashed through my mind. I could hear the kids shouting, *"Fight! Fight! Fight!"* I could see Sister Kevin approaching and handing Mateo and me a pair of boxing gloves—her face revealing her revulsion, as if they were dead rats. I could hear her telling us, *"We only have one set. So, you have to decide who's going to use the left one and who's going to use the right one."*

I headed in that direction and caressed the swing on which I had so often sat and swung, laughing and enjoying the moment with my best friend, Londri.

Then I turned towards the water tower. I stopped under it and glanced up. This was where we often congregated to discuss the issues of the day. We were completely and utterly convinced that we knew exactly how to solve all the challenges our frail planet faced, you see. We knew far better than those old farts who masqueraded as our leaders.

I went over to the tree where I had run into Favian and Marshall on that monumental day when I had just returned from the dentist—the day Favian, Marshall, and I bonded in friendship. I could see Marshall grabbing the toy soldier from my hand and declaring ceremoniously that it was "a saber-toothed tiger tooth!"

What a day that was.

I placed my hand on that tree, just as I had placed a hand on the lamppost outside our house in Cuba. I pledged the same vow: *I shall return.*

But deep down, just like that day in Cuba, I knew that this was a final farewell. I just didn't want to accept it. I was in shock and denial. There was a tightness in my throat, and my heart felt heavy. That's how I felt when I was with Alex in that place in the Florida City camp where they kept abandoned, rusted old trucks.

That was a year ago.

Many years later, I learned that shock, denial, and acceptance were three of the five stages of grief introduced by Elisabeth Kübler Ross, a Swiss-American psychiatrist. This is precisely what I was going through.

I sauntered towards *la Casa del Diablo*, the Devil's House, and hid behind the bushes where I could have some privacy: where no one could see me—where I could express my heartbreak.

And there, I wept bitter tears of grief.

That night, I lay in bed in a state of restlessness, looking back at the trajectory of events that had led Norma and me up to this point.

My brain was flooded with memories.

◉ ◉ ◉

LOOKING BACK

One of these memories was of a visit to Coney Island.

Yes, in Havana we had a Coney Island. It was spelled and pronounced the same way as it is spelled and pronounced in English, with a silent *s* in the word *island*. However, Castro didn't like the name. It sounded too Yankee—too "imperialistic," as he was wont to refer to anything having to do with the United States. Hence, the appellation was changed to *Isla del Coco*. I guess the translation would be something like "Coconut Island" or "Boogie Man Island." I think that the latter makes more sense.

Anyway, Mom and Dad took Norma and me to Coney Island a couple of times. Most of my recollections of Dad are from when I was three years old. Nevertheless, I do have fleeting memories of him from the age of two.

One day in particular comes to mind. My dad wanted me to go on one of the amusement rides by myself. Mom did not like the idea. She wanted us all to go on the ride together, but that was impossible since Norma was too little. Somehow he convinced Mom that I was old enough to go alone and that I would be okay.

"Besides," he said to her, "it's good for his development." Whatever that meant.

She caved in, reluctantly.

He picked me up and plunked me down on one of the seats. I don't know what to call that ride. It resembled a Ferris wheel, except that it moved in a horizontal rather than vertical motion, and it undulated up and down. Also, it was much faster.

I remember exactly what happened next. I decided, just for the heck of it, to slip down under the seat, where my parents could not see me. I have no idea what came over me; I was well aware that my parents would be freaked out by this, but I decided to do it anyway. It wasn't my fault. The little devil was to blame, you see.

The desired effect was accomplished. It did freak my parents out, especially my mom. She kept running in the direction of the ride, trying to follow its trajectory, wondering if something had happened to me. From a small aperture on the bottom of the seat, I observed my mom running frantically, full of anxiety.

I loved it! I thought it was so cool.

When my mom started screaming my name in desperation, I realized that what I was doing was not so funny after all. I stood so they could see me, smiled weakly, and waved at them. Then I sat on my seat to show them that I was safe and sound.

They exhaled in relief.

The ride came to a stop, and my mom came running to me. She picked me up out of the seat, hugged me and kissed me, and asked me if I was okay.

"Yes, Mami, I'm fine."

"Thank God!" she exclaimed. She held me by the shoulders and shook me. "Don't you ever do that again!"

"I'm sorry, Mami," I said and hung my head in repentance. She hugged me again. I felt really bad for having done that. But in spite of my guilt, I giggled to myself, quietly.

My restless mind on my last night at the orphanage next took me to my grandfather, the patriarch of the family.

He always made it a point to watch the evening news on television. He sat very close to the TV to get a better view because of his poor vision. I was too young to be interested in the news broadcast, but I truly enjoyed his company, especially when it was just the two of us. I loved how he responded to the news anchor, who greeted the TV viewers by saying, "Good evening to you all."

My grandfather always responded, very seriously and very respectfully, "Good evening to you, sir."

◉ ◉ ◉

INSOMNIA

Realizing that I would not succumb to slumber anytime soon, I got up and slowly meandered up the rows of beds, watching my friends sleep, hearing the soft murmur of youthful snoring. As on my last full day in Cuba, I wanted to say goodbye to my buddies without actually using words. Being present to them was my farewell.

I gazed at Londri, who was sound asleep. *Farewell, my dear friend. May our paths cross again.*

Unfortunately, they never did. I've made several attempts to locate him—all for naught.

After a few minutes, it hit me that I seriously needed to catch a little snooze of my own.

I returned to my bed and took another shot at catching forty winks.

But my thoughts would not depart me; they took me to Baldor.

◉ ◉ ◉

BALDOR

Baldor was the name of the school in Havana in which Norma and I were enrolled. It was founded by Mr. Baldor himself, a tall and impressive-looking man. Aurelio Ángel *Baldor* de la Vega was his full name. He was a mathematician, educator, lawyer, and author. He had published a popular secondary-school textbook titled *Algebra*.

Baldor was well regarded and highly respected by the nation. I once saw him getting interviewed on TV on a particular issue, along with a panel of intellectuals and experts, but I can't remember the topic. I had been watching television with my grandfather when Baldor's image appeared on the screen. I shouted excitedly, "Hey, Abuelo, that's Mr. Baldor! I go to school with him!" I quickly corrected myself. "I mean, I go to his school!"

Many years later, I ran into Mr. Baldor when I was a sophomore at Saint Peter's College in Jersey City, New Jersey. He was a mathematics professor there, known for sneaking away into an empty classroom, out of sight, so that he could work on mathematical problems in private. That's where I found him—in an empty classroom.

I coughed softly to make my presence known and dared to enter the chamber where he was busy calculating. I introduced myself in Spanish. "Buenos días, Señor Baldor."

He glanced up at me and responded, "Good morning to you, too, young man."

"You may not remember me at all, but you may remember my mother."

We spoke briefly, and he did recall speaking to my mother about getting my sister and me registered in his school.

"You have a special mother, young man," he proclaimed. "She's an inspiration to us all."

"Thank you so much for your kind words, Mr. Baldor. Yes, I know that she is special."

Prior to Saint Peter's College, he had been working as a math teacher in a private high school in New Jersey. In fact, one of my friends had Mr. Baldor as a math teacher in that school.

A once wealthy man, Baldor now drove an old car; I think it was a Ford. He, too, was a victim of the revolution. As he had done with so many people, Fidel Castro took practically everything away from Mr. Baldor—but not his dignity.

◉ ◉ ◉

MY MOM, THE SORCERESS

Thinking about Baldor, leaving the orphanage, and our imminent reunion with my mother, it was logical that my thoughts would then revert to her. By tomorrow, Norma and I would be with our mom once more.

What an unfathomable and wild journey this had been! It all started with Norma and me leaving Cuba, settling in and living temporarily in a camp for refugee children in Florida City, and on to Saint Vincent's Orphanage—in Indiana, of all places! Not only did we learn to speak English fluently, but we did a little bit of growing up as well. And we did all of this in a little less than fourteen short months.

How did all of this happen?

Simple. It was magic.

My mother was a magician, you see.

This wizardry started when a young widow with two small children decided that they needed to attend a prominent school. And she actually had the nerve to approach a very important and powerful man—someone who could place her children in one of Havana's finest schools, with a full scholarship and door-to-door, home-to-school bus service: none other than Mr. Baldor himself.

She did not make an appointment with him. She just knocked on his office door. His secretary told her that there was absolutely no way she could see him without an appointment. Furthermore, she was told that he was so busy that she would have to wait months to be granted an audience with him. Besides, school was about to begin, and she would not be able to get her children registered for the beginning of the school year. This was devastating news for my mom. Her eyes welled up.

As luck, or Providence, would have it, Mr. Baldor happened to exit his office. He saw his secretary speaking to a lady. The lady was in tears. Mr. Baldor wanted to know what was happening.

My mom tried to explain but was too emotional to speak. Mr. Baldor invited her to step into his office where they could speak in private and asked his secretary to bring her a glass of water.

My mom gave him her pitch. She told Mr. Baldor that she had long admired him for his kindness and because he was such a good Catholic. She was impressed by the way he was always willing to help those in need. She explained that her children were in need of a good education and she was hoping that they could attend his school, given its fine reputation.

"But there's a catch, Mr. Baldor," my mom explained. "I am a widow and have very little money."

Mr. Baldor was so impressed by her story that he told her, "Don't worry about the money, Nona. Starting tomorrow, your children will attend my school on a full scholarship. A bus will pick them up at home and take them back home. We will also supply them with uniforms and textbooks."

CHAPTER XV

Reunion

We were awakened very early in the morning on April 30, 1963. It was still dark outside. Sister Cordelia took me to the refectory, and as usual, Norma was already there waiting for me. We were given a farewell breakfast, and we bid a tearful adieu.

Father was there as well. He led us outside to the car, followed by quite a number of nuns. Taking our luggage, he positioned it in the trunk. "I can't take you to the airport. I have to say Mass"—he looked at his watch—"in a little over an hour. But we have provided a driver."

Father opened the rear doors for us. We entered the car, waved goodbye to him and the nuns, eyes full of tears, and off we went to Evansville Regional Airport.

In the car, Norma murmured in my ear, "I didn't get much sleep last night."

"Neither did I."

I have no memories of the car ride to the airport. We must have dozed off.

When we boarded the plane, a stewardess led us to our seats. As had transpired on the plane from Havana to Miami, she said, "Let me help you with those," fastened our seat belts, and handed us two brown paper bags, saying, "In case you need them."

This time, we didn't need the brown paper bags. Maybe we were getting used to air travel.

As the plane took off, I kept thinking about our forthcoming reunion with our mom. I said to Norma, "This is going to be just like in the movies."

I extended my hands, making a rectangle with my fingers to indicate a movie screen.

"Can't you just see us, Norma?" I brought my hands closer to us, then farther away, then closer to us again, mimicking the motion of a film camera zooming in and out. "There we are," I continued, "walking down a long airport corridor. Look, Norma! Can't you just see us? And then we notice the figure of a woman in the distance. It's Mom! She sees us, too! We go running to her, and she comes running to us. When we get to her, we just throw ourselves right onto her! Then we all hug and kiss each other. Can't you just see us?"

Norma glanced at me and smiled feebly.

And you know what? That's exactly how it happened.

☉ ☉ ☉

On the plane, the stewardesses fell in love with us. They pampered us with their attention.

"You're too skinny!" one of them told me as she grasped my upper arm.

"You sure are!" another one said, adding, "We have to fatten you up, honey!"

"Oh, no," I objected. "Don't do that!"

"Please, don't," Norma agreed.

They wouldn't have it.

"Here you go, little darlings!" The first stewardess handed us each a piece of apple pie.

"They taste better with this." Another provided us with milk. Norma and I accepted the glasses and thanked them.

"Wait a minute!" The first one slapped a scoop of vanilla ice cream on top of each pie. "Now you're cooking with gas!"

What a weird expression! I thought.

Norma looked at me and asked, "Are you hungry, Tony?"

"Not really."

"Say, honey child!" the first one protested. "Whoever told you that you have to be hungry to enjoy a little apple pie?"

Norma and I looked at each other for an instant and shrugged. We grabbed our forks and knives and gazed in wonderment at the two pieces of apple pie and ice cream in front of us.

"Go ahead! Dig in!"

So we did.

As soon as we took the first bite, the third stewardess was anxious for our opinion. "Well, whatta ya think?"

Through a mouthful of chewing, we nodded our approval. "Delicious!"

The three ladies giggled. Then they just stood there, arms crossed, smiling and watching us eat. As soon as we were finished with our apple pies, the second one offered us another treat.

"Try some of these!" She placed a plateful of pastries on my tray.

The first one said, "They taste better with butter, honey."

The third stewardess spoke. "Let me help you with that." And she started spreading butter on the sweets.

It became obvious that their attention was primarily focused on me—I guess because I was a boy. Norma didn't seem to mind.

"Ah!" the second one interjected, holding a jar of apricot marmalade. "This makes it even better!" She beamed from ear to ear as she applied a generous portion of the yummy preserve on our sweet treats.

For the most part, we just nibbled. There was no way we could have eaten the whole thing; besides, we had no such intention.

All of a sudden, one of the stewardesses underscored the reality of the situation. "Listen, ladies, we have to get back to work! There are passengers out there who need our attention!"

The first one addressed Norma and me. "Sorry, kids, but we gotta go." She chuckled. "We are supposed to be working!"

And with that, the three of them went about their business, giggling and snickering to themselves.

I don't remember much more about the voyage, except that Norma and I were exhausted, and we were certainly glad to have a little time for ourselves.

"I didn't get much sleep last night."

"Yes, Norma, you already told me that."

"Well, I'm telling you again!" She gave me a comically serious look.

"In that case, I'm telling you again as well: me neither."

She spoke incorrect English on purpose. "And I'm telling you one more time again as well, too, I don't get to sleep too much last night too!"

Norma was enjoying this bantering as much as I was.

"I know." I tried mimicking her speech—evidence that our English was quite fluent by now. "Lemme told you something for you, too." I smirked. "Like, you told me that already, like, one more time again, as well, too."

"So? You got a problem with that?"

"Well, well, well! Listen to you—such tough talk! Whatever happened to my *little* sister?"

"She grew up."

"Ha! So you're all grown up all of a sudden, is that right? Look at you, a nine-year-old woman!"

"Who's the bowling champion?" She really knew how to tease me. "You?"

"No, Norma, *you* are the bowling champion."

"And who's the one who kept throwing gutter balls?"

"All right, it was me. I admit it. I'm the one. Okay? But that was in the beginning. I got better."

"Really? How many trophies did you get?"

"Boy, you really know how to lay it on thick."

"That's right! I'm the one with the trophies! And you know what, *big* brother? I'm bringing my trophies home with me to prove it!"

"I give up, Norma. You won this round. Now let us get some sleep. Okay?"

"Just remember that *I* am the champion."

"Good night, Norma."

"Good night, *big* brother."

We both closed our eyes, and before we knew it, we were off to Snoozeville. The sugar spike from all the confectioneries may have also contributed to our weariness.

We must have slept for a long time. We were awakened by the pilot's announcement over the loudspeaker. "We are now flying over Newark Metropolitan Airport and will soon be landing. It's a cloudy day. The temperature is about fifty-five degrees."

◉ ◉ ◉

THE LONG AIRPORT CORRIDOR

I don't remember landing or getting our luggage. What I do remember is walking down a very long corridor. In the distance we saw a man and a woman heading in our direction.

"Do you think that's Mom, Tony?"

"I'm not sure." I squinted to get a better view. "Maybe."

"Who's the man?" Norma wanted to know. "Do you think that's Benny?"

"Uh." I strained my eyes even more. "Perhaps."

It wasn't. The man was Mr. Silva, the landlord of the apartment building where our mom had rented: a two-story house with four units. Looking at the house from the street, he and his wife lived on the first floor on the right side, and we lived on the second floor on the left side. Mr. and Mrs. Silva were Portuguese but were also fluent in Spanish and English.

As we approached the two figures, Norma exclaimed, "I think that lady *is* Mom!"

I wasn't so sure.

At first, Mom wasn't so sure it was us, either—after all, we had grown. Suddenly, the three of us realized what our eyes were revealing.

Yes! It was Mom!

We started running to each other, arms extended. We had to cover quite a distance! I had the sensation of running down that long corridor in slow motion.

Mom stretched her arms wide in order to receive us. Norma and I threw ourselves on top of her—just like I had imagined. Mr. Silva stayed back, smiling.

My mom exclaimed, "My dear children! Finally!" And the three of us started hugging and kissing each other.

Just like in the movies.

EPILOGUE

Spring of 1963

Mom, Norma, and I settled in Newark, New Jersey, arriving there on Tuesday, April 30, 1963. Our apartment was located two blocks from Saint Antoninus Church, which had a grammar school. We were visited the next morning by a gentleman, a social worker from the Catholic Welfare Bureau, and he escorted the three of us to Saint Antoninus School, run by the Sisters of Charity. We met the principal in her office, and she registered us. With less than two months left in the school year, it was somewhat late to get us signed up, but the principal accepted us as new students—with the assistance of the social worker, I'm sure. It probably helped that he worked for the Catholic Welfare Bureau.

Saint Antoninus School was racially integrated. Most of the white students, if not all, were Catholic. As far as I can recall, most of the African American students were Protestant, but their parents enrolled them at Saint Antoninus believing that their children would receive a better education in a Catholic school than a public one.

The nuns and priests took a liking to Norma and me and helped us as much as they could, offering us odd jobs here and there for which we were paid. The fact that we were refugees from a Communist country possibly had a lot to do with it. That Norma and I spoke English fluently was a plus. I was active in the church, becoming an altar boy once again and joining the Boy Scouts.

This was the Newark of 1963, and I remember it as a pleasant, quiet town. In a few years, Newark would regrettably be embroiled in the race riots of 1967 and 1968. But at the time, it seemed quite nice. We made new friends and liked it there.

SPRING 1986

I did return to Saint Vincent's Orphanage—twenty-three years after leaving it, almost to the day. I had envisioned meeting with the nuns and telling them that my sister and I were Pedro Pan children and had once resided in the orphanage. I thought that maybe they would show me our files and records.

As soon as I got to the town of Vincennes, something felt amiss. I was pretty sure that I was in the right location, but the orphanage wasn't there!

I ran into a local farmer and asked him, "Where's Saint Vincent's Orphanage?"

"You're practically standing on it."

"What?"

"It was torn down about ten years ago."

"Torn down?" I was dumbfounded. "And nobody told me?"

"Well, sure looks like it, don't it?" He shook his head almost apologetically, adding, "At one time there were a lot of Cuban children there."

"Yes, I know. I was one of them."

"Well, I regret to inform you then, but there was a big fire in 1972. It was set by one of the kids. That's what they say. Anyways, they tore it down a few years later. The church and the rectory are the only buildings left standing."

Again, just like in 1963, I felt a profound sadness. I meandered and took some pictures. After a few minutes, I climbed back into my car and drove to a wooded area. And just as I had done on my last full day at Saint Vincent's, I cried bitter tears of grief where no one could see me. All I could think of were the words *the impermanence of life*.

Nothing lasts forever.

As I have mentioned, I didn't have a camera when I was in the orphanage, and there are no photographs of either Norma or me during the fourteen-month period when we resided at the Florida City camp and at Saint Vincent's Orphanage. I don't recall ever seeing a camera in those days, never mind someone taking our picture or a picture of the camp, the orphanage, or any of the children.

I am quite certain that I wrote letters to my orphanage brothers once Norma and I were living in Newark, but I can't say for sure. Is it possible that I didn't send them a letter? But why wouldn't I? Then again, why would they not write back? Is it possible that the nuns intercepted the letters? But why would they do that?

I never heard from my best friend, Londri, or from Favian or Marshall, Marco or Mateo, or any of my other orphanage brothers. Never. Ever. Again.

Nothing lasts forever.

This may sound sad, but I don't mean it that way. Life is constantly changing. We have to accept this truth and surrender to it. After all, in the end, all we have is this present moment.

And for that we must be grateful.

Reflecting on this fourteen-month period of my life, I am humbled by the generosity and kindness of Father Bryan Walsh, the State Department of the United States, and the numerous other individuals and organizations that made Operation Pedro Pan a reality. The journey upon which Norma and I embarked can only be described as a miraculous voyage.

I am grateful to those who toiled in the camp at Florida City, taking care of us. And I am especially grateful to the nuns at Saint Vincent's Orphanage, and to Father, our priest, coach, and driver.

For these and all other individuals and organizations, I am grateful.

For the life they made possible for us in our new country, I am grateful.

For the honor of being a Pedro Pan kid, I am grateful.

And for this present moment, I am grateful.

ACKNOWLEDGMENTS

First of all, I have to thank my wife, Pat, for her patience and encouragement, and for putting up with me during these years of trial and error as I struggled with this memoir. I can't think of anyone better with whom to travel this journey we call life.

Special mention goes to Daniel Francis, for his indefatigable help and patience in launching a dinosaur like me into the new, breathtaking and magical world we call social media. Dan, I couldn't have done it without you!

Sal Umana also deserves mention, as well as the members of the three MILL groups (Molloy Institute for Lifelong Learning), especially Marie Giordano, president of MILL 2.

Others who should be mentioned are Roshi Robert Kennedy; SJ, the head of Morning Star Zendo Sangha; as well as Ellen and Charles Birx, for their reassurance and support.

I also need to mention those who lead the various writers' workshops to which I belong: Barbara Novack, Terri Riccardi, James Cunningham, and others.

Of course, I must express my gratitude to John Köehler, Publisher and President of Köehler Books, and all of the staff at Köehler Books who guided me along the way – Lauren Sheldon, Anna Torres, Hannah Woodlan, Joe Coccaro, the editors and artists who worked so diligently to assemble such a marvelous-looking book.

Finally, special thanks to Brian Spangle from the Knox Public Library in Vincennes, Indiana, in procuring photos of St. Vincent's Orphanage. Last but not least: Operation Pedro Pan Group, Inc., a national charitable organization founded in 1991 with the intent to connect with all Pedro Pan children who were exiled in the United States, giving us an opportunity to share our experiences.

AUTHOR BIOGRAPHY

Tony Dora is a retired teacher of ESL to Adults. Prior to becoming a teacher, Tony worked for the New York Catholic Archdiocese as Director for Spanish Language Communications, producing and directing nationally syndicated TV and radio programs. Tony also worked as a newswriter for WNJU-TV and Worldwide Television News (a subsidiary of ABC TV). He has freelanced on and off-camera directing and acting in commercials. As a member of various organizations, Tony has performed as a public speaker before a national audience. Some of his short stories, as well as excerpts from this work have been published in various college magazines, such as *Psuche* from Saint Peter's University in Jersey City, New Jersey, *Musings*, *Reflections* and others.

At an earlier time, Tony was a commissioned officer in the U.S. Air Force, where he worked as a Chaplain Candidate ministering to the troops. At the time, he was a seminarian studying to be a Roman Catholic priest. He was ordained deacon and worked in a parish, where he prepared and delivered homilies.

APPENDIX

1962-1963 BASKETBALL SCORES
12 GAMES PLAYED, 12 GAMES LOST

	OPPONENT	UNIFORM COLOR	COMMENTS
Game 1: 48-28	Saint John's	Red	A team made up of giants. They won the championship that year.
Game 2: 32-10	Saint Lawrence	Black	Another team made up of giants. They finished second that year
Game 3: 29-22	Saint Francis	Purple	This team didn't have giants. They were our closest rival.
Game 4: 15-5	Saint Joseph	Gray	The first game of a double-header, featuring fourth and fifth graders
Game 5: 28-13	Saint Joseph's	Gray	The second game featured sixth to eighth graders. We had two seventh and no eighth graders
Game 6: 45-9	Sacred Heart	Yellow	Another team made up of giants. They finished third that year
Game 7: 41-14	Saint Thomas	Dark Blue	Games seven and nine ended by the same score: 41-14. They finished fourth.
Game 8: 63-7	Saint John's	Red	The last five games were a rematch against our first four opponents.
Game 9: 41-14	Saint Lawrence	Black	Games seven and nine ended by the same score: 41-14.
Game 10: 21-14	Saint Joseph's	Gray	This was the first game of a double-header, featuring fourth and fifth graders
Game 11: 28-15	Saint Joseph's	Gray	The second game featured sixth to eighth graders. We had two seventh and no eighth graders
Game 12: 22-20	Saint Francis	Purple	A heartbreaker. With two minutes left, we were actually leading 20-18.

Saint John's won the championship that year, beating Saint Lawrence.
Sacred Heart finished in third place, beating Saint Thomas.
Towards the end of the season, Saint Francis trailed Saint Lawrence 24-21; Favian whispered, "Come on, Saint Francis!" Saint Francis lost, 36-24.
Saint Francis finished in fifth place, sealing our fate as the last-place team.
We played four games against Saint Joseph's, but they were not in our league.

www.ingramcontent.com/pod-product-compliance
Lightning Source LLC
Chambersburg PA
CBHW020524080526
44583CB00013B/723